MW01400973

NAIMAT & RAZIA KHAN
11 HOWSON CRES
EDMONTON, ALBERTA
T5A 4T7

Sharā'ṭ-e-Bai'at aur Aḥmadī kī Dhimmidāriyāṅ

Conditions of Bai'at
&
Responsibilities of an Aḥmadī

Ḥaḍrat Mirzā Masroor Aḥmad
Khalīfatul Masīḥ V

Conditions of Bai'at and Responsibilities of an Aḥmadī

(According to the Holy Qur'ān, *Aḥādīth* of the Holy Prophet Muḥammad[sa] and sayings of the Promised Messiah[as])

English translation of:

Sharā'ṭ-e-Bai'at aur Aḥmadī kī Dhimmidāriyāń Az rū'i Qur'ān, Aḥādīth aur Irshādāt-e-Ḥaḍrat Aqdas Masīḥ-e-Mau'ūd 'alaihis-Salām

Explained by: Ḥaḍrat Mirzā Masroor Aḥmad, Khalīfatul Masīḥ V[aba]

Translated by: Translation Team Jamā'at-e-Aḥmadiyyah USA.

First published in Urdu in the United Kingdom in 2004 as:
Sharā'ṭ-e-Bai'at aur Aḥmadī kī Dhimmidāriyāń.

Present English translation published in the United Kingdom in 2005.

Published by:

Islām International Publications Ltd.
"Islāmabad"
Sheephatch Lane
Tilford, Surrey GU10 2AQ, UK

Printed in the United Kingdom at:

"Islāmabad"
Raqeem Press
Tilford, Surrey GU10 2AQ, UK

ISBN: 1 85372 769 5

TABLE OF CONTENTS

Abbreviations vii

Transliteration ix

Glossary xi

Foreword xix

Promised Messiah xxi

The Author xxiii

The Conditions of Bai'at xxv

INTRODUCTION, 1

What is Bai'at? 1

Bai'at Means Handing Over One's Life to Almighty Allah 2

Divine Commandment to Take Bai'at 6

Aims and Objectives of Bai'at 8

Beginning of the System of Bai'at 9

CONDITION I, 13

Almighty Allah Will Not Forgive Shirk 13

Diverse Forms of Shirk 15

CONDITION II, 19

Falsehood—the Greatest of Evils 19
Keep Away From Adultery 26
Keep Away From the Trespasses of the Eye 27
Keep Away From Wickedness and Immorality 31
Keep Away From Cruelty 34
Keep Away From Dishonesty 38
Keep Away From Mischief 39
Keep Away From the Ways of Rebellion 41
Do Not be Carried Away by Passion 43

CONDITION III, 49

Observe Five Daily Prayers 49
Be Regular in *Tahajjud* 55
Be Very Regular in Sending *Durūd* Upon the Holy Prophet Muḥammad[sa] 58
Be Regular in *Istighfār* 62
Istighfār and Repentance 66
Always Express Gratitude to Allah 67

CONDITION IV, 75

Adopt Forgiveness and Forbearance 77
Do Not Cause Harm to Anyone 79
Adopt Meekness and Humility 85

CONDITION V, 89

Sufferings of a Muslim Are an Expiation for Sins 91

Real Time to Show Patience is When the Tragedy Strikes.. 92

You Are the Last Jamā'at Established by Allah 95

Those Who Belong to the Promised Messiah, Cannot be Separated From Him.. 97

Steadfastness 98

CONDITION VI, 101

Evolving Innovations and Rituals Deserve to be Rejected ... 105

The Holy Qur'ān is Our Guide to Islāmic Teachings........... 108

Your Life lies in the Holy Qur'ān... 110

CONDITION VII, 119

Next to *Shirk*, There is No Calamity Like Arrogance 119

Arrogant Shall Never Enter Paradise.................................... 125

Deep Connection Between Arrogance and Satan................. 127

Arrogance is Most Displeasing in the Sight of Allah 130

Status of the Meek in the Eyes of the Holy Prophet Muḥammad[sa].. 134

CONDITION VIII, 137

Essence of Islāmic Teachings 139

Revival of Islām Demands a Ransom from Us..................... 141

Means of Obtaining Salvation From Sin—Certainty of Faith.. 143

CONDITION IX, 147

Kind Treatment to All 148
The Promised Messiah[as] and His Concern for Humanity 162

CONDITION X, 167

Definition of *'Ma'rūf'* and '*Ghair Ma'rūf*' 171
Superior Example of Obedience 177
Whatever Promised Messiah[as] Attained was by Following the Holy Prophet Muḥammad[sa] 179
Submission Under All Circumstances 184
Who Enters the Jamā'at 186
Develop Brotherhood and Love Among Yourselves and a True Relationship With Allah the Almighty 188
Two Benefits of Bai'at at the Hands of Promised Messiah[as] 190
The Promised Messiah[as]—the Strong Fort of Protection for Our Times 191

Index of Names 195
Verses of the Holy Qur'ān, (chapter index) 197
Subject Index 199

ABBREVIATIONS

The following abbreviations have been used. Readers are requested to recite the full salutations:

sa *ṣal-lallāhu 'alaihi wa sallam*, meaning "may the peace and blessings of Allah be upon him" is written after the name of the Holy Prophet Muḥammad[sa].

as *'alaihis salām*, meaning "may peace be upon him" is written after the names of Prophets other than the Holy Prophet Muḥammad[sa].

ra *raḍi-Allāho 'anhu/'anhā/'anhum*, meaning "may Allah be pleased with him/her/them" is written after the names of the Companions of the Holy Prophet Muḥammad[sa] or of the Promised Messiah[as].

rta *raḥmatullāh 'alaih*, meaning "may Allah shower His mercy upon him" is written after the names of deceased pious Muslims who are not Companions of the Holy Prophet Muḥammad[sa] or of the Promised Messiah[as].

aba *ayyadahullāhu ta'ālā bi naṣrihil 'azīz*, meaning "may Allah support him with His Mighty Help" is written after the name of the current *Khalīfah* of the Promised Messiah[as].

TRANSLITERATION

This book uses the following system of transliteration adopted by the Royal Asiatic Society.

ا at the beginning of a word, pronounced as *a*, *i*, *u* preceded by a very slight aspiration, like *h* in the English word *honour.*

ث *th*, pronounced like *th* in the English word *thing*.

ح *ḥ*, a guttural aspirate, stronger than *h*.

خ *kh*, pronounced like the Scotch *ch* in *loch*.

ذ *dh*, pronounced like the English *th* in *that*.

ص ṣ, strongly articulated *s*.

ض *ḍ*, similar to the English *th* in *this*.

ط *ṭ*, strongly articulated palatal *t*.

ظ *ẓ*, strongly articulated *z*.

ع ‘, a strong guttural sound, the pronunciation of which must be learnt by the ear.

غ *gh*, a sound approached very nearly the *r* in the French *grasseye* and also the German *r.* It requires the muscles of the throat to be in the gargling position whilst pronouncing it.

ق   *q*, a deep guttural *k* sound.

ء   ', a sort of catch in the voice.

Short vowels are represented by *a* for ـَـ (like *u* in *bud*); *i* for ـِـ (like *i* in *bid*); *u* for ـُـ (like *oo* in *wood*); the long vowels by *ā* for ـَا or آ (like *a* in *father*); *i* for ـِی or ـِا (like *ee* in *deep*); *ai* for ـَی (like *i* in *site*); *ū* for ـُو (like *oo* in *root*): *au* for, ـَو (resembling *ou* in *sound*).

Please note that in transliterated words the letter *e* is to be pronounced as in *prey* which rhymes with *day*; however the pronunciation is flat without the element of English diphthong. If in Urdu and Persian words *e* is lengthened a bit more it is transliterated as *ei* to be pro-nounced as *ei* in *feign* without the element of diphthong thus کے is transliterated as *Kei*. For the nasal sound of *n* we have used the symbol *ń*. Thus Urdu word میں would be transliterated as *meiń*.[1]

The consonants not included in the above list have the same phonetic value as in the principal languages of Europe.

1. These transliterations are not included in the system of transliteration by Royal Asiatic Society.

GLOSSARY

Allah—Allah is the personal name of God in Islām. To show proper reverence to Him, Muslims often add *Ta'ālā*, 'the Most High', when saying His Holy name.

Adhān—The formal call for Islāmic daily Prayers.

Aḥādīth—Plural of *ḥadīth*, *See* **Ḥadīth**.

Aḥmadī Muslim or an Aḥmadī—A member of the Aḥmadiyyah Muslim Jamā'at.

Aḥmadiyyah Muslim Jamā'at—(Also Aḥmadiyyah) The Community of Muslims who accept the claims of Ḥaḍrat Mirzā Ghulām Aḥmad[as] of Qādiān as being the Promised Messiah and Mahdī; the Jamā'at established by Ḥaḍrat Mirzā Ghulām Aḥmad[as] in 1889, now under the leadership of his fifth *Khalīfah*, Ḥaḍrat Mirzā Masroor Aḥmad[aba].

Al-Imām al-Mahdī—The title given to the Promised Reformer by the Holy Prophet Muḥammad[sa]; it means guided leader.

Āmīn—May Allah make it so.

Asfal-us-Sāfilīn—The lowest of the low.

Assalāmo 'Alaikum—Peace be unto you. An Islāmic salutation.

Bai'at—Oath of allegiance to a religious leader; initiation at the hands of a Prophet or his *Khalīfah*.

Bukhārī—A book of *aḥādīth* (the sayings) of the Holy Prophet Muḥammad[sa] compiled by Ḥaḍrat Imām Muḥammad Bin Ismā'īl Bukhārī[rta] (194H-256H). This book of *aḥādīth* is believed to be the most authentic book after the Holy Qur'ān.

Chandah—Monetary contributions or donations.

Dajjāl—A term in Arabic that literally means, 'the great deceiver.' In Islāmic terminology '*Dajjāl*' refers to those satanic forces that would be unleashed in the Latter Days to oppose the Promised Messiah[as] and *al-Imām al-Mahdī*. A similar prophecy in the Christian faith about the appearance of the Antichrist refers to the same phenomenon, and we have therefore translated the term '*Dajjāl*' as 'Antichrist'.

Durūd—Invocation of blessings upon the Holy Prophet Muḥammad[sa].

Du'ā'—Prayer or supplication.

'Īd—A Muslim feast day; Islāmic celebration at the end of Ramaḍān and at the conclusion of Pilgrimage.

Ghaḍḍ-e-Baṣar—A term in the Holy Qur'ān that literally means 'keeping the eyes cast down'.

Ghafara—A term in the Holy Qur'ān that literally means 'covering and suppressing'.

Ḥadīth—A saying of the Holy Prophet Muḥammad[sa]. The plural is *aḥādīth*.

Ḥaḍrat—A term of respect used for a person of established righteousness and piety.

Ḥajj—Pilgrimage to the House of Allah in Mecca, Saudi Arabia; also known as the fifth pillar of Islām.

Ḥalāl—Lawful, permissible or pure.

Ḥarām—Unlawful, forbidden or impure.

Ḥaq-Mehr—The money [or gift] a husband either gives or promises to give to his wife. The amount is announced at the time of *nikāḥ*.

Holy Prophet[sa]—A term used exclusively for Ḥaḍrat Muḥammad[sa], the Prophet of Islām.

Holy Qur'ān—The Book sent by Allah for the guidance of mankind. It was revealed to the Holy Prophet Muḥammad[sa] over a period of twenty-three years.

Ḥuḍūr—Your Holiness; His Holiness.

Ijtimā'—Gathering of members of an organisation. Plural is *ijtimā'āt*.

Imām—The Arabic word for a leader. The head of the Aḥmadiyyah Muslim Jamā'at is also referred to as the *Imām*.

Inshā' Allah—An Arabic term meaning 'God-willing'.

Istighfār—Seeking Allah's forgiveness.

Istikhārah—A special Prayer made to seek guidance from Allah before making an important decision.

Jalsah-Sālānah—Annual convention or gathering.

Jamā'at—Jamā'at means community. Although the word Jamā'at itself may refer to any community, in this book,

Jamā'at specifically refers to the Aḥmadiyyah Muslim Jamā'at.

Jizyah—A tax paid by non-Muslims living in a Muslim State in lieu of military service.

Kalimah Shahādah—The declaration of the Islāmic faith: to bear witness that there is none worthy of worship except Allah, He is One, without any associate, and to bear witness that the Holy Prophet Muḥammad[sa] is His servant and His Messenger; also known as the first pillar of Islām.

Khalīfah—Caliph is derived from the Arabic word *Khalīfah*, which herein means the successor. *Khulafā'* is the plural of *Khalīfah*. In Islāmic terminology, the title 'Khalīfa-e-Rāshid' [righteous Khalifāh'] is applied to one of the first four *khulafā'* who continued the mission of the Holy Prophet Muḥammad[sa]. Aḥmadī Muslims refer to each successor of the Promised Messiah[as] as Khalīfatul Masīḥ.

Khalīfatul Masīḥ II—Ḥaḍrat Khalīfatul Masīḥ II, Mirzā Bashīr-ud-Dīn Maḥmūd Aḥmad[ra], was the second successor of the Promised Messiah[as]. He is also called Muṣleḥ-e-Mau'ūd (Promised Son) because he was born in accordance with the prophecy made by the Promised Messiah[as] in 1886 concerning the birth of a righteous son who would be endowed with unique abilities and attributes.

Khalīfatul Masīḥ IV—Ḥaḍrat Khalīfatul Masīḥ IV, Mirzā Ṭāhir Aḥmad[rta] (1928–2003), was the fourth successor of the Promised Messiah[as]. He was the grandson of the

Founder of the Aḥmadiyyah Muslim Jamā'at, Ḥaḍrat Mirzā Ghulām Aḥmad, the Promised Messiah[as].

Khalīfatul Masīḥ V—Ḥaḍrat Khalīfatul Masīḥ V, Mirzā Masroor Aḥmad[aba], is the fifth successor of the Promised Messiah[as] and the current Imām of Jamā'at-e-Aḥmadiyyah. He is the great grandson of the Promised Messiah[as].

Khilāfat—The institution of successorship in Islām.

Khuddām-ul-Aḥmadiyyah—An organisation of Aḥmadīs between the ages of fifteen and forty years.

Khulafā'—Plural of *Khalīfah, See* **Khalīfah**.

Kufr—A term in Arabic that literally means 'disbelief'.

Lajnah Imā'illāh—An organisation of Aḥmadī women above the age of fifteen years.

Mahdī—'The guided one.' This is the title given by the Holy Prophet Muḥammad[sa] to the awaited Reformer of the Latter Days.

Maulānā or Maulavī—A Muslim religious cleric.

Nikāḥ—The announcement of marriage in Islām.

Mullah—A Muslim religious cleric.

Muttaqī—A term in Arabic that literally means 'righteous person'.

Nafs—A term in Arabic that literally means 'self'.

Nafs-e-'Ammārah—A term in the Holy Qur'ān that literally means 'the self that incites to evil'.

Nawāfil—Optional or supererogatory Prayers.

(The) Promised Messiah—This term refers to the Founder of the Aḥmadiyyah Muslim Jamā'at, Ḥaḍrat Mirzā Ghulām Aḥmad[as] of Qādiān. He claimed that he had been sent by Allah in accordance with the prophecies of the Holy Prophet Muḥammad[sa] concerning the coming of *al-Imām al-Mahdī* and Messiah from among the Muslims.

Purdah—From the Hindi term *parda*, which literally means 'veil'; a state of seclusion or concealment.

Rak'at—One unit of formal worship prescribed in Islām. Plural of *rak'at* is *rak'āt*.

Rukū'—The bowing down position in the Prayer.

Ṣāḥib—A term of respect for a man, similar to the diversity of English terms like *mister* or *sir*.

Ṣadaqah—Charity or alms.

Salām—An Islāmic salutation of peace.

Ṣalāt—Five daily Prayers that are obligatory for Muslims.

Ṣalāt-ul-Witr—Three *rak'āt* of Prayer offered either at the end of *'Ishā'* Prayer or *Tahajjud* Prayer.

Sharī'ah—Islāmic religious law.

Shirk—Associating partners with Allah.

Ṣūfi—An Islāmic mystic.

Sunnah—Traditions of the Holy Prophet Muḥammad[sa] of Islām.

Sūrah—A term in Arabic referring to a chapter of the Holy Qur'ān.

Tablīgh—Preaching or propagating the message of Islām and Aḥmadiyyat. Literally means conveying (the message).

Tahajjud Prayer—Optional Prayer of great merit offered in the latter part of the night; pre-dawn formal Islāmic worship.

Taqwā—A term in Arabic that literally means 'righteousness'.

Tauḥīd—The fundamental Islāmic belief that there is none worthy of being worshipped except Allah.

'Ulema—A class of Muslim scholars.

Ummah—The larger community of Muslims.

Walīmah—Reception given by the husband after the marriage has been consummated.

Waṣīlah—Intermediation, intercession.

Zakāt—A term in Arabic that literally means 'increase' or 'purification'; technically signifies the obligatory alms prescribed in Islām.

FOREWORD

By the immense grace and mercy of Allah the Almighty, we have been blessed to accept the Promised Messiah and Mahdī Ḥaḍrat Mirzā Ghulām Aḥmad[as] of Qādiān, whose advent was prophesied by the Holy Prophet Muḥammad[sa]. *Alḥamdolillah.* When the Promised Messiah[as] was granted permission by Allah to take *bai'at*, he published an announcement called *Ishtihār Takmīl-e-Tablīgh* on January 12, 1889, which mentions the Ten Conditions of Bai'at. Anyone who joins the Jamā'at of the Promised Messiah[as] pledges to abide by these Conditions. It is essential for all followers of the Promised Messiah[as] to understand the details of these Conditions and to strive to follow them.

For our guidance and benefit, Ḥaḍrat Mirzā Masroor Aḥmad, Khalīfatul Masīḥ V[aba], has eloquently explained these conditions of *bai'at* in light of the Holy Qur'ān, *Aḥādīth* of the Holy Prophet Muḥammad[sa] and sayings and writings of the Promised Messiah[as]. Ḥuḍūr[aba] discussed the first three conditions of *bai'at* in his concluding address at the Annual Convention of the Aḥmadiyyah Muslim Jamā'at, UK, on July 27th 2003. In his concluding address at the Annual Convention of the Aḥmadiyyah Muslim Jamā'at, Germany on August 24, 2003, Ḥuḍūr[aba] explained the fourth, fifth and sixth conditions of *bai'at*. On August 29, in his Friday Sermon, Ḥuḍūr[aba] explained the seventh and eighth conditions of *bai'at* in Frankfurt, Germany. The ninth condition was addressed in his Friday sermon on September 12, 2003 at the Faḍl Mosque in

London. Finally, the tenth condition of *bai'at* was addressed in his Friday sermon on September 19, 2003 at the Faḍl Mosque in London.

These speeches and sermons were delivered by Ḥuḍūr[aba] in Urdu, and after his additional revisions, were published in book form in July 2004. This translation has been prepared by the Translation Team of Jamā'at-e-Aḥmadiyyah USA, headed by Munawar A. Sa'eed, working under the direction of Vakālat-e-Taṣnīf London. The translators are: Dr. Faḍl Aḥmad, Dr. Khalīl Malik, Mubashar Aḥmad and Munawar A. Sa'eed. Important contributions in finalizing the document were made by Amjad M. Khān, 'Abdul-Wahab Mirzā and several other members of the team. May Allah the Almighty reward all of them abundantly, (*Āmīn*).

May Allah the Almighty enable us to understand truly and to abide by these Conditions faithfully, and may He enable us to become true Aḥmadīs as the Promised Messiah[as] desired. (*Āmīn*).

It should be noted that the 'new edition' of *Malfūẓāt* refers to the edition published recently in five volumes from Qādiān. References to *Malfūẓāt* that do not specify 'new edition' refer to the edition published in the United Kingdom in 1984; and references to the books of the Promised Messiah[as] are all based on the United Kingdom Edition.

Munīr-ud-Dīn Shams
Additional Vakīl-ut-Taṣnīf
July 2005

THE PROMISED MESSIAH[AS]

The worldwide Aḥmadiyyah Muslim Jamā'at was founded in 1889. Its Founder, Ḥaḍrat Mirzā Ghulām Aḥmad [may peace be on him] of Qādiān, India, claimed to be the Promised Reformer whose advent was awaited under different names and titles by the adherents of various religions. Under Divine guidance, Ḥaḍrat Mirzā Ghulām Aḥmad[as] revealed that only one such reformer was to appear and that his mission was to bring mankind into the fold of a single universal religion, Islām. He also maintained that the Promised Reformer was to appear as a subordinate and follower of the Holy Prophet of Islām, Ḥaḍrat Muḥammad [may peace and blessings of Allah be upon him]—in accordance with the prophecies by him about the second coming of Messiah and the appearance of *al-Imām, al-Mahdī*. He claimed to be the person in whom these prophecies were fuflilled.

THE AUTHOR

Ḥaḍrat Mirzā Masroor Aḥmad, Khalīfatul Masīḥ V[aba], is currently the supreme head of the worldwide Aḥmadiyyah Muslim Community. He is the fifth successor and great grandson of the Promised Messiah and Reformer, Ḥaḍrat Mirzā Ghulām Aḥmad[as] of Qādiān. He was elected to this position in London, England by an electoral college on April 22, 2003, a few days after the death of his predecessor, Ḥaḍrat Mirzā Ṭāhir Aḥmad, Khalīfatul Masīḥ IV[rta].

Ḥaḍrat Mirzā Masroor Aḥmad did his primary education at Ta'aleem-ul-Islām High School Rabwah, and obtained his BA from Talīm-ul-Islām (TI) College Rabwah, Pakistan. In 1976 he earned his Masters of Science degree in Agricultural Economics from the Agriculture University Faisalabad, Pakistan.

Prior to his being elected as Khalīfah, Ḥaḍrat Mirzā Masroor Aḥmad[aba] accumulated an impressive record of humanitarian services that underscore his commitment to education and philanthropy. His altruistic endeavours took him to Ghana in 1977 where, for several years, he served as a principal of various Aḥmadiyyah Muslim schools. He helped to inaugurate the Aḥmadiyyah Secondary School Salaga, where he served as principal for the school's first two years.

Ḥaḍrat Mirzā Masroor Aḥmad[aba] was able to make use of the knowledge of his studied discipline, agricultural economics, to carry out research about wheat production in Ghana. The first successful experiment of planting, growing and nurturing wheat as an economic crop in Ghana was exhibited at an international trade fair and the results were submitted to the Ministry of Agriculture of Ghana.

In December of 1997, Ḥaḍrat Mirzā Masroor Aḥmad[aba] was appointed to the office of Nāẓir-e-A'alā (chief executive director) of the Ṣadr Anjuman Aḥmadiyyah Pakistan. In 1999, Ḥaḍrat Mirzā Masroor Aḥmad[aba] was falsely charged with blasphemy and wrongly accused of defaming verses of the Holy Qur'ān. He was arrested and imprisoned for eleven days in his hometown of Rabwah until it was shown that the charges brought against him were entirely unfounded.

Ḥaḍrat Mirzā Masroor Aḥmad[aba] currently resides in London, England. As spiritual leader of Aḥmadī Muslims all over the world, he vigorously champions the cause of Islām through a refreshing message of peace and compassion.

TEN CONDITIONS OF BAI'AT

Initiation Into the Aḥmadiyyah Muslim Jamā'at

I

The initiate shall solemnly promise that he/she shall abstain from *shirk* [associating any partner with God] right up to the day of his/her death.

II

That he/she shall keep away from falsehood, fornication/adultery, trespasses of the eye, debauchery, dissipation, cruelty, dishonesty, mischief and rebellion; and that he/she will not permit himself/herself to be carried away by passions, however strong they might be.

III

That he/she shall regularly offer the five daily Prayers in accordance with the commandments of God and the Holy Prophet Muḥammad[sa] and shall try his/her best to be regular in offering the *tahajjud* and invoking *durūd* on the Holy Prophet Muḥammad[sa]. That he/she shall make it his/her daily routine to ask forgiveness for his/her sins, to remember the bounties of God and to praise and glorify Him.

IV

That under the impulse of any passions, he/she shall cause no harm whatsoever to the creatures of God in general and Muslims in particular, neither by his/her tongue, hands, nor any other means.

V

That he/she shall remain faithful to God in all circumstances of life, in sorrow and in happiness, in adversity and in prosperity, in felicity and in trial; and that he/she shall in all conditions remain resigned to the decree of God and keep himself/herself ready to face all kinds of indignities and sufferings in His way and shall never turn away from Him at the onslaught of any misfortune; on the contrary, he/she shall march forward.

VI

That he/she shall refrain from following un-Islāmic customs and lustful inclinations and shall completely submit himself/herself to the authority of the Holy Qur'ān; and that he/she shall make the Word of God and the sayings of the Holy Prophet Muḥammad[sa] his/her guiding principles in every walk of his/her life.

VII

That he/she shall entirely give up pride and vanity and shall pass all his/her life in humbleness, cheerfulness, forbearance and meekness.

VIII

That he/she shall hold faith, the honour of faith and the cause of Islām dearer to his/her life than wealth, honour, children, and all loved ones.

IX

That he/she shall keep himself/herself occupied in the service of God's creatures for His sake only and shall endeavour towards the beneficence of mankind to the best of his/her God-given abilities and powers.

X

That he/she shall enter into a bond of brotherhood with this humble servant of God, pledging obedience to me in everything good for the sake of God, and remain faithful to it until the day of his/her death. That he/she shall exert such a high devotion in the observance of this bond as is not to be found in any other worldly relationship and connection that demand devoted dutifulness.

INTRODUCTION

[From the concluding address delivered at the Annual Convention of the Aḥmadiyyah Muslim Jamā'at, United Kingdom, on July 27, 2003, in which first three conditions of bai'at were explained in detail.]

Some members of the Jamā'at have written to me saying that: 'We have renewed our *bai'at* [pledge of initiation] at your hand and have pledged to abide by the conditions of *bai'at*, but we do not have full awareness and knowledge of those ten Conditions.'

I thought that I should address this subject on the occasion of the Annual Convention[1] today. Since the subject is long I cannot cover all conditions now but I will only cover a few. I will *inshā' Allah* continue this subject in a subsequent Friday sermon or some other occasion.

What is Bai'at?

The first question is: What is *bai'at*? To explain it, I will quote some *aḥādīth* of the Holy Prophet Muḥammad[sa] and sayings of the Promised Messiah[as].

---

1. Reference is to the concluding address delivered at the Annual Convention of the Aḥmadiyyah Muslim Jamā'at, United Kingdom on July 27, 2003, in which first three conditions of *bai'at* were explained in detail.

The Promised Messiah[as] says:

> *Bai'at* truly means to sell oneself; its blessings and impact are based on that condition. Just as a seed is sown into the ground, its original condition is that the hand of the farmer has sown it, but it is not known what will happen to it. If the seed is of a good quality and possesses the capacity to grow, then with the grace of Allah the Almighty, and as a consequence of the work done by the farmer, it grows until one grain turns into a thousand grains. Similarly, the person taking *bai'at* has to first adopt lowliness and humility and has to distance himself from his ego and selfishness. Then that person becomes fit for growth. But he who continues to hold on to his ego, along with taking *bai'at*, will never receive any grace. (*Malfūẓāt*, vol. 6, p. 173)

Bai'at Means Handing Over One's Life to Almighty Allah

The Promised Messiah[as] further says:

> To take *bai'at* means handing over your life to Almighty Allah. It means, 'Today we have sold our life to Almighty Allah.' It is wrong to say that by treading in the path of Allah anybody would ultimately suffer a loss. The truthful can never be in a state of loss. Only he who is false—i.e., who, for worldly gain, breaks the pledge that he has made with Almighty Allah—suffers loss. One who commits such an action because of the fear of the world should remember that at the time of his death no ruler or king of this world would come to procure his release. He has to present himself to the Judge of all the

> judges, Who will enquire of him, 'Why did you not honour Me?' Therefore, it is essential for all the believers to believe in Allah, Who is the King of the heavens and earth and to make a true repentance. (*Malfūẓāt*, vol. 7, p. 29–30)

These sayings of the Promised Messiah[as] make it very obvious what *bai'at* is. If each one of us recognises that, 'My person does not now belong to me; I now have to abide by all injunctions of Almighty Allah under all circumstances and have to follow them faithfully, and make all acts of mine subservient to the pleasure of Allah,' that would be a summary of the ten conditions of *bai'at*.

I will now present a few *aḥādīth* in which the subject of *bai'at* is treated in different ways.

> 'Iyāḍullāh Bin 'Abdullāh[ra] narrates that: 'Ubādah Bin Aṣ-Ṣāmit[ra] was among the Companions who joined the battle of Badr and also took part in *bai'at* at 'Aqabah. 'Ubādah Bin Aṣ-Ṣāmit[ra] told 'Iyāḍullāh Bin 'Abdullāh[ra] that the Holy Prophet[sa] said at the time when a group of his Companions were around him: Come and take a *bai'at* upon the condition:
>
> اَلَّا تُشْرِكُوْا بِاللّٰهِ شَيْئًا
>
> that you will not associate anything with Allah, nor will you steal, nor will you commit adultery[2], nor will you kill your children, nor will you slander, nor will you disobey me in anything good I ask you to do. So anyone of you who will prove true to this pledge of *bai'at*, his reward is with Almighty

2. The word adultery as used in this booklet covers all sexual relations outside the system of marriage.

Allah. Whoever falls short of fulfiling this pledge and suffers a loss in this world, his loss will become expiation for him. And he who falls short of fulfiling this pledge of *bai'at*, and Almighty Allah covers his faults, his affair is with Almighty Allah; if He wills, He may punish him, and if He wills, He may forgive him.' (*Ṣaḥīḥ Al-Bukhārī*, Kitābu Manāqibil Anṣāri, Bābu Wufūdil Anṣāri Ilan-Nabiyyi Bi Makkata Wa Bai'atil 'Aqabah)

Then there are other *aḥādīth*

Ḥaḍrat 'Ubādah Bin Aṣ-Ṣāmit[ra] narrates that, 'We pledged at the hand of the Holy Prophet[sa] on the condition that we will listen and obey during the times of comfort and also during the times of hardship, during periods of joy and also during periods of pain, and that we will not argue with those in authority, and wherever we might be, we will hold fast to truth and will not be afraid of the objections of any critics.' (*Saḥīḥ Al-Bukhārī*, Kitāb-ul Bai'ati, Bābul Bai'ati 'Alas Sam'i Wat Ṭā'ah)

Mother of the faithful, Ḥaḍrat 'Āishah[ra] relates that, 'The Holy Prophet[sa] used to take the pledge from the women in accordance with the verse of the Holy Qur'ān:[3]

يٰاَيُّهَا النَّبِيُّ اِذَا جَآءَكَ الْمُؤْمِنٰتُ يُبَايِعْنَكَ عَلٰٓى اَنْ لَّا يُشْرِكْنَ بِاللّٰهِ
شَيْـًٔا وَّ لَا يَسْرِقْنَ وَ لَا يَزْنِيْنَ وَلَا يَقْتُلْنَ اَوْلَادَهُنَّ وَلَا يَاْتِيْنَ بِبُهْتَانٍ يَّفْتَرِيْنَهٗ
بَيْنَ اَيْدِيْهِنَّ وَ اَرْجُلِهِنَّ وَلَا يَعْصِيْنَكَ فِيْ مَعْرُوْفٍ فَبَايِعْهُنَّ وَاسْتَغْفِرْ لَهُنَّ
اللّٰهَ. اِنَّ اللّٰهَ غَفُوْرٌ رَّحِيْمٌ.

3. Al-Mumtaḥanah, 60:13

> 'O Prophet! when believing women come to thee, taking the oath of allegiance *at thy hands* that they will not associate anything with Allah, and that they will not steal, and will not commit adultery, nor kill their children, nor bring forth a scandalous charge which they themselves have deliberately forged, nor disobey thee in what is right, then accept their allegiance and ask Allah to forgive them. Verily, Allah is Most Forgiving, Merciful.'

Ḥaḍrat 'Āishah[ra] continues that:

> At the time of taking the pledge, the hand of the Holy Prophet[sa] never touched the hand of any woman except those who belonged to his household. (*Saḥīḥ Al-Bukhārī*, Kitāb-ul-Aḥkami, Bābu Bai'atin Nisā'i)

Even before the Promised Messiah[as] started taking *bai'at*, some pious Muslims were troubled by the conditions which had fallen upon Islām and felt that the only person who could save the ark of Islām from drowning and who had true sympathy for Islām was Ḥaḍrat Mirzā Ghulām Aḥmad Qādianī[as], and that he was the *al-Imām* and *al-Mahdī*. Therefore, people used to request of him to take their pledge, but he always responded:

لَسْتُ بِمَامُوْرٍ

'I have not been commissioned.' He once wrote to Maulavī 'Abdul Qādir Ṣāḥib[ra], care of Mīr 'Abbās 'Alī Ṣāḥib, that:

> The nature of this humble one is overpowered with the Unity of God and committing all affairs to Allah, and… since Almighty Allah has not conveyed anything to me in the

matter of *bai'at*, it is not proper that I should do so on my own initiative.

لَعَلَّ اللّٰهَ يُحْدِثُ بَعْدَ ذٰلِكَ اَمْرًا [4]

Maulavī Ṣāḥib should continue to strive to foster the brotherhood in faith and nurture this tree with the pure water of sincerity and love; this method will God-willing prove beneficial. (*Ḥayāt-e-Aḥmad*, vol. 2, No. 2, p. 12–13)

Divine Commandment to Take Bai'at

After six to seven years, in the first quarter of year 1888, Almighty Allah commanded the Promised Messiah[as] to take *bai'at*. The divine commandment was conveyed in the following words:

اِذَا عَزَمْتَ فَتَوَكَّلْ عَلَى اللّٰهِ وَاصْنَعِ الْفُلْكَ بِاَعْيُنِنَا وَوَحْيِنَا– اَلَّذِيْنَ يُبَايِعُوْنَكَ اِنَّمَا يُبَايِعُوْنَ اللّٰهَ يَدُاللّٰهِ فَوْقَ اَيْدِيْهِمْ

(*Ishtihār*, December 01, 1888, p. 2)

That is:

> And when you made up your mind, then trust Allah. And, make an ark before Our eyes and according to Our revelation. Those who take a pledge at your hand take a pledge with Allah. Allah's hand is above their hands.

---

4. It is possible that the Almighty Allah may reveal something later.

The Promised Messiah[as], because of his nature, disliked that all types of people should join in his *bai'at*. His heart-felt desire was that only such blessed people whose nature was firmly established on fidelity should join this blessed Jamā'at. Therefore, he waited for an occasion that should distinguish between those who were faithful and those who were hypocrites. Allah the Most Glorious, through His perfect wisdom and mercy, created that occasion in the same year in November 1888 by the death of Bashīr I (who was the son of the Promised Messiah[as]). As a consequence, there was a huge commotion raised against him. Many people of weak faith separated themselves from him. The Promised Messiah[as] considered this an appropriate occasion to start the Aḥmadiyyah Muslim Jamā'at. On December 1st 1888, he made a general announcement for *bai'at*. The Promised Messiah[as] also directed that those who come for *bai'at* should first perform *istikhārah*[5], according to the traditions of the Holy Prophet Muḥammad[sa]. (*Ishtihār Takmīl-e-Tablīgh*, Jan 12, 1889)

That is to say, they should first pray, then perform *istikhārah*, and then take *bai'at*.

After publishing this announcement, the Promised Messiah[as] moved from Qādiān to Ludhiana and stayed at the house of Ḥaḍrat Ṣūfī Aḥmad Jān in Maḥalla Jadīd. (*Ḥayāt-e-Aḥmad*, vol. 3, Part I, p. 1)

---

5. A special Prayer made to seek guidance from Allah before making an important decision.

Aims and Objectives of Bai'at

From Ludhiana, the Promised Messiah[as] published another announcement, on March 4th 1889, explaining the aims and objectives of *bai'at*. He said:

> This system of *bai'at* has been established solely to gather together a group of the righteous people in a Jamā'at so that a weighty group of the righteous people should make a holy impact on the world. The unity of these righteous people should be a source of blessings, grandeur, and positive results for Islām. The blessings of being united on one creed may enable them to perform noble and righteous services for the sake of Islām. They may not be lazy, stingy, and useless Muslims; nor should they be like the unworthy ones who have done great damage to Islām because of their discord and disunity; nor such as have vitiated Islām's beautiful countenance with their unholy conditions; nor should they be like those heedless dervishes and hermits who have no awareness of what Islām needs, nor have any sympathy for their brothers, nor have any enthusiasm to do good deeds for humanity. Rather, they should be such sympathisers of the nation that they should become a refuge for the poor and fathers for the orphans. In the service of Islām, they should be willing to sacrifice themselves like one overpowered with love. All their efforts should be devoted to spread Islām's blessings throughout the world so that a pure fountain of the love of Allah and sympathy for humanity may flow from every heart and, being combined in one place, should look like a flowing river.... Almighty Allah desires to manifest His Glory and

demonstrate His Omnipotence through this group, and then He desires to grant it further progress so that the world may be filled with the love of Allah, true repentance, purity, true goodness, peace, reconciliation, and sympathy for mankind. This group will be a special group of Allah, and He will grant them power through His Own spirit, and He will safeguard them from unholy life, and He will bring about a pure change in their life. As He has promised in His holy glad tidings, He will increase this group tremendously and thousands of the truthful will join it. He Himself will irrigate it and make it prosper until its numbers and blessings will be a source of marvel for all who see. Like a lamp placed high, they will spread their light on all sides of the world, and they will be considered an example of the blessings of Islām. Allah will grant all kinds of blessings to the perfect followers of this Movement, and He will grant them victory over all others. Upto the Day of Judgement, there will be people among them who will be granted Divine acceptance and succour. This is what the Glorious God has desired; He is All-Powerful and does what He desires. All strength and power belong to Him. (*Tablīgh-e-Risālat*, vol. 1, p. 150–155)

In the same announcement, the Promised Messiah[as] said that those who wish to make *bai'at* should arrive in Ludhiana after March 20, 1889.

Beginning of the System of Bai'at

In accordance with the above announcement, the Promised Messiah[as] took the pledge of allegiance on March 23, 1889 at the house of Ḥaḍrat Ṣūfī Aḥmad Jān Ṣāḥib located in Maḥalla Jadīd. As narrated by Ḥaḍrat Munshī 'Abdullāh[ra] of Sanour, a register was prepared to record this historical event. It was called *bai'at* for repentance, seeking righteousness and purification.

In those days, the Promised Messiah[as] used to invite people one by one to take *bai'at* in a room and then he took *bai'at* from each person individually. The first person whose *bai'at* was accepted was Ḥaḍrat Maulānā Nūr-ud-Dīn[ra]. Admonishing those who took this *bai'at*, the Promised Messiah[as] said:

> By joining this Jamā'at, you should bring about a complete transformation in your former life so that you have true faith in Allah, and He becomes your Helper in all calamities. You should not take His ordinances lightly, but should rather honour every one of His commandments and prove such honour in your actions.
>
> To turn towards worldly means for various reasons and to place your trust in them instead of trusting Allah amount to making partners with Allah, as if you were denying the existence of God. You should consider worldly means only to the extent that they do not amount to associating partners with Allah. My way is that I do not forbid you from using the worldly means, but I do forbid you from placing your trust in them. Your hand should be engaged in work, but your heart should be attached to the True Beloved.

He also said:

> All of you who have taken *bai'at* and have made a commitment, listen! To utter these words is easy, but to do justice to them is hard because Satan is always busy trying to make man

careless about his faith. Satan shows the world and its benefits to be within reach, and faith to be distant. In this way, the heart is hardened and each subsequent condition is worse than the previous one. If you want to please Allah, put your entire strength and effort to abide faithfully to this commitment of freeing yourself from sins.

He also said:

Utter no words of mischief, spread no evil, bear the rebukes with patience, do not confront anyone, even if someone confronts you, and deal with him with kindness and goodness. Demonstrate a good example of sweetness of conversation. Abide by all commandments with a true heart so that Allah be pleased with you and even the enemy may recognise the change in you after *bai'at*. Give true evidence in court cases. All those who join this Movement should establish themselves on truthfulness with full heart, full endeavour, and the entirety of life. (*Dhikr-e-Ḥabīb*, p. 436–439)

In March 1903, on the day of 'Eīd, some Companions[ra] were sitting together and the Promised Messiah[as] said:

Listen all of you who have taken *bai'at* today[6] and those who have taken *bai'at* before, I would like to say a few words by way of advice. Listen to them carefully. *Bai'at* that you have taken today is *bai'at* of repentance. Repentance is of two types. One from the previous sins. That is, to reform oneself from the mistakes committed before and to make recompense as far as possible to

6. It seems that at that time people had gathered together to take *bai'at*.

set right the damage done by them. The second is to safeguard oneself from sins thereafter and to save oneself from the fire.

Almighty Allah has promised that with repentance all prior sins are forgiven provided that the repentance is made with a true heart and pure intent and does not contain any secret mischief in any corner of the heart. Allah knows the hidden secrets of the hearts; He cannot be misled by anyone. Do not try to mislead Him. Make repentance in His presence with truthfulness, not hypocrisy. The repentance is not something extra or useless for man. Its impact is not limited to the Day of Judgement; rather, it straightens both worldly affairs and the faith. The repentant achieves peace and prosperity, both in this life and in the life to come. (*Malfūẓāt*, vol. 5. p. 187–188)

CONDITION I

The initiate shall solemnly promise that he/she shall abstain from shirk [associating any partner with God] right up to the day of his/her death.

Almighty Allah Will Not Forgive Shirk

Allah the Almighty says in *sūrah* al-Nisā', verse forty-nine:

اِنَّ اللّٰهَ لَا يَغْفِرُ اَنْ يُّشْرَكَ بِهٖ وَيَغْفِرُ مَادُوْنَ ذٰلِكَ لِمَنْ يَّشَآءُ . وَمَنْ يُّشْرِكْ بِاللّٰهِ فَقَدِ افْتَرٰٓى اِثْمًا عَظِيْمًا

'Surely, Allah will not forgive that any partner be associated with Him; but He will forgive whatever is short of that to whomsoever He pleases. And whoso associates partners with Allah has indeed devised a very great sin.'

The Promised Messiah[as] says in this respect that:

Similarly, Allah has said in the Holy Qur'ān:

وَيَغْفِرُ مَا دُوْنَ ذٰلِكَ ...الخ

This means that every sin is forgivable except *shirk*. Therefore, do not go near *shirk* and consider it to be a forbidden tree. (*Ḍamīmah Toḥfah-e-Golarhviyyah*, *Rūḥānī Khazā'in*, vol. 17, p. 323–324, footnote)

Then the Promised Messiah[as] says:

Shirk here does not merely mean bowing before stones, etc.; rather, it is also *shirk* that you should depend entirely on worldly means and emphasise worldly idols. This is what *shirk* is. (*Al-Ḥakam*, vol. 7, No. 24, June 30, 1903, p. 11)

Then Almighty Allah says in the Holy Qur'ān:[7]

وَاِذْ قَالَ لُقْمٰنُ لِابْنِهٖ وَهُوَ يَعِظُهٗ يٰبُنَيَّ لَا تُشْرِكْ بِاللّٰهِ . اِنَّ الشِّرْكَ لَظُلْمٌ عَظِيْمٌ

And *remember* when Luqmān said to his son while exhorting him, 'O my dear son! associate not partners with Allah. Surely, associating partners *with God* is a grievous wrong.'

The Holy Prophet[sa] feared *shirk* in his *ummah* [followers]. One *ḥadīth* states:

'Ubādah Bin Nasī told us about Shaddād Bin 'Aus that he was crying. He was asked, 'Why do you cry?' He replied, 'I have remembered something that I heard from the Holy Prophet[sa] and it has made me cry. I heard the Holy Prophet[sa] say that, "I fear about *shirk* and their secret desires in my *ummah*." I asked, "O Prophet of Allah, will your people be involved in *shirk* after you?" The Holy Prophet[sa] responded, "Yes, even though

7. Luqmān, 31:14

my people will not worship the Sun and the Moon, the idol and the stone, they will suffer from ostentations in their actions and they will be prey to their hidden desires. One of them will start the day fasting but then he will come across a desire and he will break the fast and indulge in his desire.'" (*Musnadu Aḥmadabni Ḥanbal*, vol. 4. p. 124, printed in Beirut)

Diverse Forms of Shirk

It is clear from this *ḥadīth* that even if one does not indulge in manifest *shirk* of worshipping idols or the Moon, resorting to ostentation and following one's desires are also forms of *shirk*. If an employee exceeds the limits of due obedience to his employer, and by way of flattery praises him and believes that his sustenance depends on him, that too is a form of *shirk*. If someone is proud of his sons and believes that he has so many sons who are growing up and would gain employment, make earnings and take care of him, or that none of his collaterals would be able to compete with him because of his grown sons, that too is *shirk*. (In the Indian subcontinent, rather in the entire third world, such competition with collaterals is a loathsome habit.) Such people rely entirely upon their sons who turn out to be disobedient, or die in accidents, or become disabled; the entire support of such people thereby falls to the ground.

The Promised Messiah[as] says:

> *Tauḥīd* [Unity of God] does not simply mean that you say *lā ilāha illallāh*[8] with your tongue but then hide hundreds of idols

8. There is none worthy of worship except Allah.

in your heart. Anyone who gives reverence to his own plans, mischief or clever designs as he should revere God, or depends upon another person as one should depend upon God alone, or reveres his own ego as he should revere God alone, in all such conditions he is an idol-worshipper in the sight of Allah. Idols are not merely those that are made of gold, silver, copper or stones. Rather, every thing, every statement, or every deed, which is revered in a manner that befits Almighty Allah alone, is an idol in the sight of Allah.... Remember that the true Unity of God, which God requires us to affirm and upon which salvation depends, is to believe that God in His Being is free from every associate, whether it be an idol or a human being, or the Sun or Moon, or one's ego, or one's cunning or deceit; it is also to conceive of no one as possessing power in opposition to Him, nor to accept anyone as Sustainer, nor to hold anyone as bestowing honour or disgrace, nor to consider anyone as Helper or Supporter; and it is also to confine one's love to Him and one's worship, and one's humility, and one's hopes, and one's fear to Him. No Unity can be complete without the following three types of particularisation. First, there is the Unity of Being—that is, to conceive the whole universe as nonexistent in contrast with Him and to consider it mortal and lacking reality. Secondly, the Unity of Attributes—that is that *Rabūbiyyat* [Lordship] and *Ulūhiyyat* [Godhead] are confined to His Being and that all others who appear as sustainers or benefactors are only a part of the system set up by His hand. Thirdly, the Unity of love, sincerity and devotion—that is, not to consider anyone as an associate of God in the matter of love and worship and to be entirely lost in Him. (*Sirāj-ud-Dīn 'Īsā'ī ke Chār Swāloṅ kā Jawāb, Rūḥānī Khazā'in*, vol. 12, p. 349–350)

I have briefly explained this before. In this respect, Ḥaḍrat Khalīfatul Masīḥ I[ra] says:

> To associate anyone in the name, action, or worship of Allah constitutes *shirk*, and to carry out all good deeds solely for the pleasure of Allah is called worship. People believe that there is no Creator except Allah, and they also believe that life and death are in the hands of Allah Who has complete control and power over them. Eventhough they believe in this, they prostate in front of others, tell lies, and perform circuits before others. Instead of worshipping Allah, they worship others, instead of fasting for Allah, they fast for others, and instead of praying to Allah, they pray to others and give alms for them. To uproot these false notions, Almighty Allah raised the Holy Prophet Muḥammad[sa]. (*Khuṭabāt-e-Nūr*, p. 7–8)

CONDITION II

That he/she shall keep away from falsehood, fornication/adultery, trespasses of the eye, debauchery, dissipation, cruelty, dishonesty, mischief and rebellion; and that he/she will not permit himself/herself to be carried away by passions, however strong they might be.

Nine kinds of sins are mentioned in this condition, and the initiate, everyone who claims to belong to the Jamā'at of the Promised Messiah[as], should eschew those sins.

Falsehood—the Greatest of Evils

Indeed, falsehood is the greatest of all evils. Once someone asked the Holy Prophet[sa] for advice because that person was suffering from many weaknesses and did not think that he could leave all of them at once. The Holy Prophet[sa] told him, 'Promise that you will always speak the truth and will never tell a lie.' Just by adopting the path of truthfulness, he was freed from all of his sins one by one. Whenever he thought of committing a sin, he thought that if he were caught he would be presented before the Holy Prophet[sa]. He had promised not to tell a lie. If he were to speak the truth [about the act], he might be humiliated or punished. Gradually, he was freed from all his sins. Indeed, falsehood is the root of all evils.

I will now elaborate upon this further. Almighty Allah says in the Holy Qur'ān:[9]

ذٰلِكَ وَمَنْ يُّعَظِّمْ حُرُمٰتِ اللّٰهِ فَهُوَ خَيْرٌ لَّهٗ عِنْدَ رَبِّهٖ وَاُحِلَّتْ لَكُمُ الْاَنْعَامُ
اِلَّا مَا يُتْلٰى عَلَيْكُمْ فَاجْتَنِبُوْا الرِّجْسَ مِنَ الْاَوْثَانِ وَاجْتَنِبُوْا قَوْلَ الزُّوْرِ

That is *God's commandment*. And whose honours the sacred things of Allah, it will be good for him with his Lord. And cattle are made lawful to you but not that which has been announced to you. Shun therefore the abomination of idols, and shun false speech.

Here, uttering falsehood has been mentioned together with *shirk*. Then Allah says:[10]

اَلَا لِلّٰهِ الدِّيْنُ الْخَالِصُ. وَالَّذِيْنَ اتَّخَذُوْا مِنْ دُوْنِهٖ اَوْلِيَآءَ مَا نَعْبُدُهُمْ اِلَّا
لِيُقَرِّبُوْنَآ اِلَى اللّٰهِ زُلْفٰى. اِنَّ اللّٰهَ يَحْكُمُ بَيْنَهُمْ فِىْ مَا هُمْ فِيْهِ يَخْتَلِفُوْنَ. اِنَّ
اللّٰهَ لَا يَهْدِىْ مَنْ هُوَ كَاذِبٌ كَفَّارٌ

Hearken, it is to Allah *alone* that sincere obedience is due. And those who take for protectors others beside Him *say*, 'We serve them only that they may bring us near to Allah in station.' Surely, Allah will judge between them concerning that

9. Al-Ḥajj, 22:31
10. Al-Zumar, 39:4

wherein they differ. Surely, Allah guides not him who is an ungrateful liar.

There is another *ḥadīth* in *Ṣaḥīḥ Muslim*:

Ḥaḍrat 'Abdullāh Bin 'Amr Bin al-'Āṣ[ra] relates that the Holy Prophet[sa] said, 'Whoever has the following four characteristics is a real hypocrite, and whoever has one of these characteristics has an element of hypocrisy until he leaves that habit:

- When he speaks, he tells a lie. [His speech is mingled with falsehood, and he utters falsehood.]
- When he makes a contract, he breaks it.
- When he makes a promise, he breaks it. [This is also a form of faslehood.]
- When he argues, he starts using foul language.'

All of these characteristics are related to the telling of lies. Then there is another *ḥadīth*.

Ḥaḍrat Imām Mālik[ra] relates that, 'I have heard that Ḥaḍrat 'Abdullāh Bin Mas'ūd[ra] used to say, "Adopt truthfulness because truthfulness leads towards virtue, and virtue leads to Paradise. Avoid falsehood because falsehood leads to disobedience, and disobedience conveys one to Hell. Do you not know that it is said that such and such spoke the truth and obeyed; or that he lied and was involved in sin?"' (*Al-Mu'aṭṭā Lil Imām Mālik*, Bābu mā jā'a fiṣ-ṣidqi wal-kadhib)

Then there is a *ḥadīth* in *Musnadu Aḥmadabni Ḥanbal*:

Ḥaḍrat Abū Hurairah[ra] relates that the Holy Prophet[sa] said, 'Whoever invited a young child to give him something and did not do so, it would be counted as a lie.' (*Musnadu Aḥmad-abni Ḥanbal*, vol. 2, p. 452, printed in Beirut)

This point is very important for moral training. Keep in mind that for the moral training of children you should not say such things even by way of jest. Otherwise, children will pick up the habit of telling lies in daily conversation, and lying would become a firm habit later in their lives. Gradually they will lose all feelings and inhibitions against telling lies.

Ḥaḍrat Ibn-e-Mas'ūd[ra] has related that the Holy Prophet[sa] said, 'Truth guides to virtue, and virtue guides to Paradise. A person keeps telling the truth till in the sight of Allah he is named truthful. Lying leads to vice, and vice leads to the Fire; and a person keeps lying till in the sight of Allah he is named a liar.' (*Ṣaḥīḥ Al-Bukhārī*, Kitābul-Adabi, Bābu Qaulillāhe Ittaqullāha wa kūnū ma'aṣ Ṣādiqīn)

Ḥaḍrat 'Abdullāh Bin 'Amr Bin al-'Āṣ[ra] narrates that, 'A man came to the Holy Prophet[sa] and said, 'O Prophet of Allah, what are the deeds that lead to Paradise?' The Holy Prophet[sa] replied, 'Speaking the truth. When a servant of Allah speaks the truth, he becomes an obedient servant, and when he becomes an obedient servant, he becomes a true believer, and a true believer finally enters Paradise.' The man asked again, 'O Prophet of Allah, what is the action that leads to Hell?' The Holy Prophet[sa] replied, 'Falsehood. When someone tells a lie, he becomes disobedient, and disobedience is *kufr* [disbelief], and someone who is established on disbelief finally enters Hell.' (*Musnadu Aḥmadabni Ḥanbal*, vol. 2, p. 176, printed in Beirut)

The Promised Messiah[as] says:

> The Holy Qur'ān has regarded the uttering of falsehood to be an abomination as Allah says:[11]
>
> فَاجْتَنِبُوْا الرِّجْسَ مِنَ الْاَوْثَانِ وَاجْتَنِبُوْا قَوْلَ الزُّوْرِ
>
> Here the words falsehood and idolatry have been used in conjunction. Indeed, falsehood is an idol because otherwise no one would leave the truth. Just as an idol has nothing but artificial polish, so too, falsehood has no reality behind it. Those who tell lies lose their credibility so much that even when they speak the truth one thinks that perhaps there is an element of falsehood in it. If those who are given to telling lies want to cut down their habits, they will not find it easy; they have to struggle for a long time before they get used to speaking the truth. (*Malfūẓāt*, vol. 3, p. 350)

The Promised Messiah[as] also says:

> Of all the natural conditions of man, one that is an essential part of his nature is truthfulness. Normally, unless a person is moved by some selfish motive, he does not wish to tell a lie. He is naturally averse to falsehood and is reluctant to have recourse to it. That is why he dislikes a person whom he knows to be a liar and looks upon him with disdain. But this natural condition by itself cannot be considered moral. Even children and the insane exhibit this quality. The fact is that so long as a person does not renounce the selfish motives which prevent him from telling the truth, he cannot be considered

11. Shun therefore the abomination of idols, and shun false speech. Al-Ḥajj, 22:31

truthful. If a person tells the truth only when he stands to lose nothing, but tells a lie when his honour, property or life are threatened, how can he be considered better than children and the insane? Do minors and the insane not speak this kind of truth? There is hardly anyone in the world who would tell a lie without any motive. Therefore, the truth that is forsaken when faced with possible loss can never form part of true morals. The real occasion of telling the truth is when one apprehends loss of life or property or honour. In this context, the Divine teaching is:

فَاجْتَنِبُوْا الرِّجْسَ مِنَ الْاَوْثَانِ وَاجْتَنِبُوْا قَوْلَ الزُّوْرِ [12]

وَلَا يَاْبَ الشُّهَدَآءُ اِذَا مَا دُعُوْا [13]

وَلَا تَكْتُمُوْا الشَّهَادَةَ وَمَنْ يَّكْتُمْهَا فَاِنَّهٗ اٰثِمٌ قَلْبُهٗ [14]

وَ اِذَا قُلْتُمْ فَاعْدِلُوْا وَلَوْ كَانَ ذَا قُرْبٰى [15]

كُوْنُوْا قَوَّامِيْنَ بِالْقِسْطِ شُهَدَآءَ لِلّٰهِ وَلَوْ عَلٰٓى اَنْفُسِكُمْ اَوِالْوَالِدَيْنِ وَالْاَقْرَبِيْنَ [16]

وَلَا يَجْرِمَنَّكُمْ شَنَاٰنُ قَوْمٍ عَلٰٓى اَلَّا تَعْدِلُوْا [17]

---

12. Al-Ḥajj, 22:31
13. Al-Baqarah, 2:283
14. Al-Baqarah, 2:284
15. Al-An'ām, 6:153
16. Al-Nisā', 4:136
17. Al-Mā'idah, 5:9

وَالصّٰدِقِيْنَ وَالصّٰدِقٰتِ [18]

وَتَوَاصَوْا بِالْحَقِّ وَتَوَاصَوْا بِالصَّبْرِ [19]

لَا يَشْهَدُوْنَ الزُّوْرَ [20]

Keep away from idol worship and lying because falsehood too is an idol; one who relies upon it ceases to rely upon God. Hence, by telling lies, one loses God.

When you are summoned to testify to the truth, do not refuse to do so.

Do not conceal true testimony; and he who conceals it, his heart is certainly sinful.

And when you speak, speak only what is absolutely true and fair, even when you testify against a close relative.

Hold fast to truth and justice, and bear witness only for the sake of Allah; never utter a lie even if telling the truth may endanger your lives or your parents' lives or other loved ones like your children.

Let not hostility towards a people prevent you from giving true testimony.

Truthful men and truthful women will earn great reward.

They are accustomed to counselling truth.

They do not keep company with the untruthful.

---

18. Al-Aḥzāb, 33:36
19. Al-'Aṣr, 103:4
20. Al-Furqān, 25:73

(*Islāmī Uṣūl kī Philosophy, Rūḥānī Khazā'in*, vol. 10, p. 360–361)

Keep Away From Adultery

The second condition of *bai'at* also includes a commitment to avoid adultery. In this respect, Almighty Allah says in the Holy Qur'ān:[21]

وَلَا تَقْرَبُوْا الزِّنٰٓى اِنَّهٗ كَانَ فَاحِشَةً. وَسَآءَ سَبِيْلًا

And come not near unto adultery; surely, it is a foul thing and an evil way.

In a *ḥadīth*, Muḥammad Bin Sīrīn narrates that the Holy Prophet[sa] admonished to do the following. Then he narrates a long *ḥadīth* that includes the admonition that chastity and truthfulness are better and everlasting in contrast to adultery and falsehood (*Sunanud-Dāra Quṭniyyi, Kitāb-ul-Waṣāyā, Bābu mā yustaḥabbu bil-waṣiyyati minat-tashahhudi wal kalām*)

Here adultery and falsehood have been mentioned together. This also illustrates how major a sin lying is.

The Promised Messiah[as] says:

Do not go near adultery. That is to say, avoid all occasions that create that thought in your mind. Avoid all ways that carry a risk of getting involved in this sin. Whoever commits adultery goes to the limit of the evil. Adultery is a very evil way. It stops you from reaching your true objective and

21. Banī Isrā'īl, 17:33

carries major risks in it. He who is unable to get married should try to maintain his chastity in other ways; for instance, he should keep fasts or reduce his food intake, or should do hard physical work. (*Islāmī Uṣūl kī Philosophy*, *Rūḥānī Khazā'in*, vol. 10, p. 342)

The Promised Messiah[as] has admonished to stay away from things that lead to adultery. Sometimes the youth ignore this matter. They get used to watching films that are not fit to be seen. They are beneath good moral standards. Avoid them because that is also a form of adultery.

Keep Away From the Trespasses of the Eye

The second condition also refers to a third kind of evil, which is the trespasses of the eye. Avoiding it is known as *ghaḍḍ-e-baṣar*[22].

Ḥaḍrat Abū Raihanah[ra] narrates that he was with the Holy Prophet[sa] in an expedition and one night heard the Holy Prophet[sa] say, 'Fire is forbidden to touch the eye that remains awake for the sake of Allah, and fire is forbidden on the eye that sheds tears for the fear of Allah.'

Ḥaḍrat Abū Shuraiḥ[ra] narrates that he heard one narrator say that the Holy Prophet[sa] also said that, 'Fire is forbidden on that eye which, instead of watching, is cast down when confronted with something that Allah has forbidden to see, and fire is also forbidden to touch the eye that has been taken out in the way

22. A term in the Holy Qur'ān, which literally means: keeping the eyes cast down.

of Allah the Glorious.' (*Sunanud-Dārimiyyi,* Kitāb-ul-Jihādi, Bābu filladhī yas-haru fī sabīlillāhi Ḥārisan)

Then there is another *ḥadīth.*

'Ubādah Bin Aṣ-Ṣāmit[ra] narrates that the Holy Prophet Muḥammad[sa] said, 'Assure me of six things concerning you, and I will assure your entry into Paradise:

- When you speak, say the truth.
- When you make a promise, fulfil it.
- When you are given a trust, convey it when demanded. [There should be no excuses.]
- Safeguard your private parts.
- Keep your eyes cast down.
- Hold your hands from cruelty.'

(*Musnadu Aḥmadabni Ḥanbal*, vol. 5, p. 323, printed in Beirut)

Ḥaḍrat Abū Sa'īd Khudrī[ra] relates that the Holy Prophet[sa] directed, 'Refrain from sitting in the streets.' It was said to him, 'Messenger of Allah, we cannot help sitting in the streets.' He said, 'In that case fulfil the obligations due to the street.' He was asked, 'What is due to the street?' He replied, 'Reciprocation of greetings, restraining of looks, guiding those who ask for directions, enjoining good and forbidding evil.' (*Musnadu Aḥmadabni Ḥanbal*, vol. 3. p. 61, printed in Beirut)

The Promised Messiah[as] writes that:

> The Holy Qur'ān, which lays down appropriate directions with reference to the natural desires and weaknesses of man, has adopted an excellent course in this regard[23]:
>
> قُلْ لِلْمُؤْمِنِيْنَ يَغُضُّوْا مِنْ اَبْصَارِهِمْ وَيَحْفَظُوْا فُرُوْجَهُمْ. ذٰلِكَ اَزْكٰى لَهُمْ
>
> Direct the believing men to restrain their looks and to guard their *furūj*. That is the act through which they will attain purification.
>
> *Furūj* does not refer merely to the private parts. It refers to all parts of the entry in the boy including the ears. It has been prohibited to hear the song of an unrelated woman. Remember, it is proven by hundreds of experiments, that if God prohibits something, man has to leave it sooner or later. (*Malfūẓāt*, vol. 7, p. 135)

The Promised Messiah[as] also says:

> Islām has enjoined men and women equally on the observations of these conditions. As women are prescribed to wear the veil, so too are men commanded to keep their eyes down. *Ṣalāt* [obligatory Prayer], fasting, *Zakāt* [obligatory alms], *Ḥajj* [Pilgrimage to the House of God in Mecca], the distinction between *ḥalāl* [lawful] and *ḥarām* [unlawful], avoiding un-Islāmic customs to honour God's commandment, are all injunctions that make the door of Islām very narrow and that

23. Al-Nūr, 24:31

is why everyone cannot enter this door. (*Malfūẓāt*, new ed., vol. 5. p. 614)

This should make it clear for men that they should keep their eyes down. Modesty is not just for women, it is also for men.

Then the Promised Messiah[as] says:

God Almighty has not only set forth excellent teachings for acquiring the quality of chastity, but has furnished man with five remedies against unchaste behaviour. These are [1] to restrain one's eyes from gazing upon women who are outside the prohibited degrees, [2] to safeguard the ears from listening to their voices, [3] to refrain from listening to the stories about them, [4] to avoid occasions that might furnish incitement towards this vice, and [5] to control oneself during the period of celibacy through fasting, dieting, etc…

We can confidently claim that this excellent teaching with all its devices that is set forth in the Holy Qur'ān is peculiar to Islām. It should be kept in mind that as the natural condition of man, which is the source of his passions, is such that he cannot depart from it without a complete change in himself; his passions are bound to be roused when they are confronted with the occasion and opportunity for indulging in this vice; therefore, God Almighty has not instructed us that we might freely gaze at women outside the prohibited degrees and might contemplate their beauty and observe all their movements in dancing, etc., but that we should do so with pure looks. Nor have we been instructed to listen to the singing of these women and to lend an ear to the tales of their beauty, but that we should do so with a pure intent. We have been positively commanded not to look at their beauty whether with pure intent or otherwise, nor to listen to their musical voices or to descriptions of their good looks, whether with pure intent or otherwise. We have been directed to eschew all this as we eschew carrion, so that we should not stumble. It is almost certain that our free glances would cause us to stumble some time or another.

As God Almighty desires that our eyes and our hearts and all our limbs and organs should continue in a state of purity, He has furnished us with this excellent teaching. There can be no doubt that unrestrained looks become a source of danger. If we place soft bread before a hungry dog, it would be vain to hope that the dog should pay no attention to it. Thus, God Almighty desired that human faculties not be provided with any occasion for secret functioning and not be confronted with anything that might incite dangerous tendencies. (*Islāmī Uṣūl kī Philosophy, Rūḥānī Khazā'in*, vol. 10, p. 343–344)

Keep Away From Wickedness and Immorality

The second condition also enjoins saving oneself from wickedness and immorality.

Almighty Allah says in the Holy Qur'ān:[24]

وَاعْلَمُوْٓا اَنَّ فِيْكُمْ رَسُوْلَ اللّٰهِ لَوْ يُطِيْعُكُمْ فِيْ كَثِيْرٍ مِّنَ الْاَمْرِ لَعَنِتُّمْ وَلٰكِنَّ اللّٰهَ حَبَّبَ اِلَيْكُمُ الْاِيْمَانَ وَزَيَّنَهٗ فِيْ قُلُوْبِكُمْ وَكَرَّهَ اِلَيْكُمُ الْكُفْرَ وَالْفُسُوْقَ وَالْعِصْيَانَ. اُولٰٓئِكَ هُمُ الرَّاشِدُوْنَ

> And know that among you is the Messenger of Allah; if he were to comply with your wishes in most of the matters, you would surely come to trouble; but Allah has endeared the faith to you and has made it *look* beautiful to your hearts, and He has made disbelief, wickedness and disobedience hateful to you. Such indeed are those who follow the right course.

In a *ḥadīth* pertaining to this subject, Ḥaḍrat Aswad[ra] narrates from Ḥaḍrat Abū Hurairah[ra] that:

> When someone is fasting, he should not indulge in foul talk, nor talk of wickedness or ignorance. If someone deals with him in ways of ignorance, he should simply respond, 'I am fasting.' (*Musnadu Aḥmadabni Ḥanbal*, vol. 2, p. 356, printed in Beirut)
>
> The Holy Prophet[sa] has also said, 'To rebuke a believer is wickedness and to fight him is disbelief.' (*Musnadu Aḥmadabni Ḥanbal*, vol. 1, p. 437, printed in Beirut)
>
> 'Abdur-Raḥmān Bin Shibl narrates the Holy Prophet[sa] said, 'The merchants are wicked.' The narrator adds that he was asked, 'Does Allah not make trade lawful?' The Holy Prophet[sa] said, 'Why not? But when they make a deal, they tell lies and raise the price making statements under oath.'

The narrator adds that:

> The Holy Prophet[sa] said, 'The wicked will be in hell.' He was asked, 'Who are the wicked?' He answered, 'Some women are wicked.' A man asked, 'Prophet of Allah, are they not our mothers, sisters, and wives?' He answered, 'Why not? But

---

24. Al-Ḥujurāt, 49:8

when something is given to them, they are not grateful; and when a hardship befalls them, they do not show patience.' (*Musnadu Aḥmadabni Ḥanbal*, vol. 3, p. 428, printed in Beirut)

The businessmen need to ponder over this. Clean dealings are a condition of *bai'at*.

The Promised Messiah[as] says:

> It is established from *ḥadīth* that the wicked should be punished before the disbelievers.... This is the way of Allah, that when a nation becomes wicked and immoral, another nation is made to rule over it. (*Malfūẓāt*, new ed., vol. 2, p. 653)

Then he says:

> When wickedness and immorality exceeded their limits, and people started disrespecting the commandments and signs of Allah, and were lost into the affairs of the world and its adornment, God caused their ruin at the hands of Halākū and Changez Khān. It is written that at that time a cry was heard from heaven:[25]
>
> اَيُّهَا الْكُفَّارُ اُقْتُلُوْاالْفُجَّار
>
> In short, the wicked and the immoral are lower and more despicable than disbelievers in the eyes of Allah. (*Malfūẓāt*, new ed., vol. 3, p. 108)

25. O disbelievers kill the transgressors.

Then he says:

The prayer of the wicked tyrant is not accepted because he is unmindful of Allah, and thus Allah cares not for him. If a son is unmindful of his obligations to his father, the father does not care about him, because of his disobedience. Why should Allah care for such people? (*Tafsīr Ḥaḍrat Masīḥ-e-Mau'ūd*[as], new ed., vol. 3, p. 611)

Keep Away From Cruelty

The second condition also enjoins avoiding cruelty. The Holy Qur'ān says:[26]

فَاخْتَلَفَ الْاَحْزَابُ مِنْ بَيْنِهِمْ فَوَيْلٌ لِّلَّذِيْنَ ظَلَمُوْا مِنْ عَذَابِ يَوْمٍ اَلِيْمٍ

But the parties differed among themselves. So woe to those who were cruel by way of the punishment of a grievous day.

Ḥaḍrat Jābir[ra] narrates that the Holy Prophet[sa] said, 'Beware of cruelty because cruelty will appear as darkness on the Day of Judgement. Beware of greediness, stinginess and envy because greediness, stinginess and envy caused the destruction of the earlier nations. It incited them to bloodshed and to dishonour that which was sacred.' (*Musnadu Aḥmadabni Ḥanbal*, vol. 3, p. 323, printed in Beirut)

To usurp the rightful belonging of others is also cruelty.

Ḥaḍrat 'Abdullāh Bin Mas'ūd[ra] narrates that, 'I asked the Holy Prophet[sa], "What is the greatest cruelty?" He said, "The

26. Al-Zukhruf, 43:66

> greatest cruelty is that a brother should unlawfully occupy one arm's length of land from his brother. On the Day of Judgement, even a pebble from the land he has usurped will be placed as a chain around his neck; and no one knows the depth of the earth except Allah Who has created it.'" (*Musnadu Aḥmadabni Ḥanbal*, vol. 1, p. 396, printed in Beirut)

Some people fail to discharge the obligations to their sisters, brothers and neighbours, or illegally occupy their properties and land. Please ponder over this. As Aḥmadīs, the conditions upon which we have taken the pledge require us not to usurp the rights of anyone, nor to be cruel. We need to fear Allah greatly about this matter.

There is a *ḥadīth* that:

> Ḥaḍrat Abū Hurairah[ra] has related that the Holy Prophet[sa] said, 'Do you know who a pauper is?' We answered, 'Among us a pauper is one who has no cash or property.' He said, 'A pauper from among my people would be one who faces the Day of Judgement with a record of *Ṣalāt* and fasting and *Zakāt*, but who will have abused one, falsely calumniated someone else, devoured the substance of a third, shed the blood of a fourth and beaten a fifth. Then each of them will be allotted a portion of his good deeds. Should they not suffice, their sins and defaults will be transferred from them to him and he will be thrown into the Fire.' (*Ṣaḥīḥ Muslim*, Kitāb-ul-Birri waṣ-Ṣilah, Bābu Taḥrīmiẓ-Ẓulmi)

Please ponder over this matter. All of us who are guilty of such misdeeds need to be fearful. May Allah safeguard every one of us from appearing in His presence in the condition of such a pauper.

The Promised Messiah[as] also says:

> The members of my Jamā'at, wherever they might be, should listen with attention. The purpose of their joining this Movement and establishing the mutual relationship of spiritual preceptor and disciple with me is that they should achieve a high degree of good conduct, good behaviour and righteousness. No wrongdoing, mischief, or misconduct should even approach them. They should perform the five daily Prayers regularly, should not utter falsehood and should not hurt anyone by their tongues. They should be guilty of no vice and should not let even a thought of any mischief, wrong, disorderliness, or turmoil pass through their minds. They should shun every type of sin, offence, undesirable action, passion, and unmannerly behaviour. They should become pure-hearted and meek servants of God Almighty, and no poisonous germ should flourish in their beings.... Sympathy with mankind should be their principle and, they should fear God Almighty. They should safeguard their tongues and their hands and their thoughts against every kind of impurity, disorderliness and dishonesty. They should join the five daily Prayer services without fail. They should refrain from every kind of wrong, transgression, dishonesty, bribery, trespass, and partiality. They should not participate in any evil company. If it should be proved that one who frequents their company does not obey God's commandments... or is not mindful of the rights of people, or is cruel or mischievous, or is ill-behaved, or is seeking to deceive the servants of God

Almighty by speaking ill or abusively of him, or is guilty of imposture towards the persons with whom they have entered into a covenant of *bai'at*, it should be their duty to repel him and to keep away from such a dangerous one. They should not design harm against the followers of any religion or the members of any tribe or group. Be true well-wishers of every one, and take care that no mischievous or vicious person, or disorderly one or ill-behaved one, should ever be of your company, or should dwell among you; for such a person could at any time be the cause of your stumbling.

These are matters and conditions that I have been urging from the beginning, and it is the duty of every member of my Jamā'at to act upon them. You should indulge in no impurity, mockery or derision. Walk upon the earth with good hearts, pure tempers, and pure thoughts. Not every evil is worth fighting, so cultivate the habit of forgiveness and overlooking defaults, and behave with steadfastness and meekness. Do not attack anyone improperly, and keep your passions under complete control. If you take part in a discussion, or in an exchange of views on a religious subject, express yourself gently and be courteous. If anyone misbehaves towards you, withdraw from such company with a greeting of peace. If you are persecuted or reviled, be mindful that you should not meet stupidity with stupidity, for otherwise you will be counted in the same category as your opponents. God Almighty desires that you should become a *jamā'at* that should set an example of goodness and truthfulness for the whole world. Hasten to exclude everyone from your company who sets an example of evil, mischief, provocation and ill-behaviour. He who cannot dwell among us in meekness, goodness and piety, using gentle words and comporting himself in ways of good conduct, should depart from us quickly, for God does not desire that such a one should dwell among us. He will die miserably, for he did not adopt the way of goodness. Therefore, be alert, and be truly good-hearted, gentle and righteous. You will be known by your regular attendance at Prayer services and your high moral qualities. He who has the seed of evil embedded in him will not be able to conform to this admonition. (*Tablīgh-e-Risālat*, vol. 7, p. 42–43. *Ishtihār*, May 29, 1898, p. 2)

Keep Away From Dishonesty

Almighty Allah says about dishonesty in the Holy Qur'ān:[27]

وَلَا تُجَادِلْ عَنِ الَّذِيْنَ يَخْتَانُوْنَ اَنْفُسَهُمْ .اِنَّ اللّٰهَ لَايُحِبُّ
مَنْ كَانَ خَوَّانًا اَثِيْمًا

> And plead not on behalf of those who are dishonest to themselves. Surely, Allah loves not one who is perfidious *and* a great sinner.

According to a *ḥadīth*:

> Ḥaḍrat Abū Hurairah[ra] narrates that the Holy Prophet[sa] said, 'If someone gives you something for safekeeping, return it to him. Do not be dishonest with anyone, even if he has been dishonest with you.' (*Sunano Abī Dāwūd*, Kitāb-ul-Buyū', Bābu fir-Rajuli ya'khudhu Ḥaqqahū…)

27. Al-Nisā', 4:108

The Promised Messiah[as] says:

> Of the various forms of discarding evil, the second is the virtue known as honesty and integrity, which is the indisposition to harm anyone by taking possession of his property mischievously and dishonestly. It should be clear that honesty and integrity constitute a natural human condition. That is why an infant, which is by nature simple and naïve, and, because of young age, has not yet acquired any bad habits, dislikes what belongs to others so much so that it is with great difficulty that [he] allows a strange woman to breastfeed [him]. (*Islāmī Uṣūl kī Philosophy, Rūḥānī Khazā'in*, vol. 10, p. 344)

Keep Away From Mischief

Almighty Allah says about mischief in the Holy Qur'ān:[28]

وَابْتَغِ فِيْمَا اٰتٰـکَ اللّٰـهُ الدَّارَ الْاٰخِرَةَ وَلَا تَنْسَ نَصِيْبَکَ مِنَ الدُّنْيَا
وَاَحْسِنْ کَمَا اَحْسَنَ اللّٰهُ اِلَيْکَ وَلَا تَبْغِ الْفَسَادَ فِی الْاَرْضِ. اِنَّ اللّٰهَ لَا
يُحِبُّ الْمُفْسِدِيْنَ

> 'And seek, in that which Allah has given thee, the Home of the Hereafter; and neglect not thy lot in this world; and do good *to others* as Allah has done good to thee; and seek not to make mischief in the earth, verily Allah loves not those who make mischief.'

Ḥaḍrat Mu'ādh Bin Jabal[ra] relates that the Holy Prophet[sa] said, 'Combat is of two types: One that is waged for the pleasure of

28. Al-Qaṣaṣ, 28:78

Allah under the leadership of an *Imām* [divinely guided leader]. A person engaged in such combat spends his best property in the way of Allah, is comforting his companions, and avoids mischief. For such a person, everything—his sleeping and waking time—earns merit in the sight of Allah. And there is another who engages in combat for pride, ostentation, and to talk about his valour. He disobeys the *Imām* and creates mischief in the earth. Such a one can never equal the first one in rank.' (*Sunano Abī Dāwūd*, Kitāb-ul-Jihād, Bābu fī man yaghzū wa yaltamis)

Ḥaḍrat Asmā' Bint Yazīd[ra] narrates that the Holy Prophet[sa] said, 'Should I inform you about the best of people?' The Companions[ra] said, 'Certainly, tell us O Prophet of Allah.' He said, 'When they witness a desirable scene, they start remembering Allah.' Then he said, 'Should I tell you about the worst of people? The worst people are those who go about backbiting and creating discord between people. Their wish is that the obedient servants of Allah get involved in sin.' (*Musnadu Aḥmadabni Ḥanbal*, vol. 6, p. 459, printed in Beirut)

The Promised Messiah[as] says:

Do not engage in fighting or discord with those who leave you because you have joined a Movement established by Almighty Allah; instead, pray for them in secret that Almighty Allah may grant them the insight and cognition that He has granted you. With your pious example and good behaviour, prove that you have adopted the right path. Listen! I am appointed to admonish you repeatedly to avoid all occasions of discord and disturbance. Have patience even if you hear abuse. Respond to evil with goodness. If you encounter discord, slip away from that situation or respond with kind words.... I do not like when I learn that someone has quarrelled despite being a member of my Jamā'at. Almighty Allah does not like that the *jamā'at* that is destined to become a model for mankind should adopt such ways, which are not the ways of righteousness. Indeed, I tell you that Almighty Allah has emphasised this matter so much that if someone—declaring his membership of the Jamā'at—does not show patience and perseverance, he does not belong to this Jamā'at. The utmost cause of your provocation might be that you hear people abusing me. Leave that matter for God to decide. You cannot judge it. Leave my affair to God; you should show patience even in the face of such abuse. (*Malfūẓāt*, new ed., vol. 4, p. 157)

Keep Away From the Ways of Rebellion

The second condition of *bai'at* also requires that the initiate shall safeguard himself from the ways of rebellion. In explaining two verses of *surāh* al-Baqarah, the Promised Messiah[as] says:[29]

وَقَاتِلُوْهُمْ حَتّٰى لَا تَكُوْنَ فِتْنَةٌ وَيَكُوْنَ الدِّيْنُ لِلّٰهِ

That is:

And fight them until the rebellion is removed, and religion is professed only for Allah.

29. Al-Baqarah, 2:194

قُلْ قِتَالٌ فِيْهِ كَبِيْرٌ وَصَدٌّ عَنْ سَبِيْلِ اللّٰهِ وَكُفْرٌ بِهٖ وَالْمَسْجِدِ الْحَرَامِ
وَاِخْرَاجُ اَهْلِهٖ مِنْهُ اَكْبَرُ عِنْدَ اللّٰهِ وَالْفِتْنَةُ اَكْبَرُ مِنَ الْقَتْلِ وَلَا يَزَالُوْنَ
يُقَاتِلُوْنَكُمْ حَتّٰى يَرُدُّوْكُمْ عَنْ دِيْنِكُمْ اِنِ اسْتَطَاعُوْا

That is:

> Fighting (in the Holy city of Mecca) is a heinous thing, but to hinder men from the ways of Allah and to be ungrateful to Him, and to expel the righteous men from the Sacred Mosque is more heinous in the sight of Allah. And rebellion, that is, interfering in the peaceful living, is worse than killing... (*Jang-e-Muqaddas*, *Rūḥānī Khazā'in*, vol. 6, p. 255)

The Promised Messiah[as] also said:

> I see that many ignorant and mischievous people from among the Hindus and Muslims demonstrate such activities against the government that smell of rebellion. I suspect that a time will come when the ways of rebellion will be established in their hearts. Therefore, I admonish the members of my Jamā'at who are settled in Punjab and [the subcontinents of] India who, by the Grace of God, number in hundreds of thousands, that they should remember this teaching of mine that I have been impressing upon them in my speeches as well as in my writings for the last twenty-six years, that they should be truly loyal to this government that has done us favours.... Remember it well that a person who entertains any rebellious thoughts against the government cannot continue to be a

30. Al-Baqarah, 2:218

member of my Jamā'at. I consider it a great impertinence that we be ungrateful to a government that delivered us from the clutches of tyrants and under which we are making progress. Almighty Allah says in the Holy Qur'ān:

هَلْ جَزَآءُ الْإِحْسَانِ إِلَّا الْإِحْسَانُ

That is: The reward for goodness is nothing but goodness.

In a *ḥadīth*, the Holy Prophet[sa] says that, 'Anyone who is ungrateful to people cannot be grateful to Allah.' Just imagine, if you move outside the protective shade of this government, where will you find refuge? Name one government that will grant you protection. Every Islāmic government is grinding its teeth to kill you because according to them you are disbelievers and apostates. Be then grateful for this favour of Allah.... To spread the doctrines that a bloody *Mahdī* will come and will apprehend all the Christian monarchs is a concocted approach that has blackened and hardened the hearts of our opposing Muslims. Such doctrines can, and definitely will, incite the ignorant to rise in rebellion at some time. Therefore, we are striving that Muslims may get rid of such doctrines. Remember, a faith that lacks human sympathy, is not from God. God has taught us, 'Be merciful on earth so that you may be shown mercy in Heaven.' (*Majmū'ah Ishtihārāt*, vol. 3, p. 582–585)

Do Not be Carried Away by Passion

The second condition also draws the initiate's attention to not being carried away by passion. The Promised Messiah[as] says:

The fourth stage of spiritual progress is that which is mentioned by Almighty Allah in the noble verse of the Holy Qur'ān:[31]

وَالَّذِيْنَ هُمْ لِفُرُوْجِهِمْ حٰفِظُوْنَ

That is, higher in status than the believers of the third rank are those who guard themselves against the carnal passions and unlawful lust. This rank is higher than the third rank because at the third rank one only sacrifices wealth that is dear to him. But a believer at the fourth rank sacrifices something that is dearer to him than wealth—the carnal passions. Man is so enamored with his carnal passions that he spends large sums to satisfy his lust. He gives no importance to wealth when pursuing such desires. It has been observed that there are many stingy people who do not give a penny to the needy, but destroy their households by spending large amounts on visiting women of ill repute. It is thus established that the carnal passions are a fierce flood that carries with it a filthy habit like stinginess. It is therefore obvious, that in comparison with the strength of faith that cures stinginess and prepares one to part with his beloved property for the sake of Allah, a much stronger and long-lasting faith in combating Satan is required to safeguard oneself from the deluge of carnal passions, because such faith tramples under its foot the old serpent called *Nafs-e-'Ammārah* [the self that incites to evil]. As far as stinginess is concerned, it can be avoided during times of satisfying the carnal passions or for ostentation and show, but this deluge that is raised by the upsurge of carnal passions is a very

31. And who guard their chastity—. Al-Mu'minūn, 23:6

severe and long-lasting deluge that cannot be averted except with the mercy of Allah. Just as the bone is the hardest part and longest living in the components of the body, so too the strength of faith needed for safeguarding from this deluge is hardest and longest lasting so that it may persist in combating this enemy for a long time. And that too with the mercy of Allah, because the deluge of carnal passions is such a devastating flood that nobody can safeguard himself from it except with the mercy of Allah. That is why Ḥaḍrat Yūsuf[as] had to say:

وَمَآ اُبَرِّئُ نَفْسِيْ. اِنَّ النَّفْسَ لَاَمَّارَةٌ بِالسُّوْٓءِ اِلَّا مَا رَحِمَ رَبِّيْ

That is:

'And I do not absolve myself of weakness; for the soul is surely prone to enjoin evil. It is not possible to safeguard oneself from its attack except that Allah the Almighty should have mercy.'

The phrase mentioned in this verse is:[32]

اِلَّا مَا رَحِمَ رَبِّيْ

Similar words were used at the time of Noah's deluge:[33]

لَاعَاصِمَ الْيَوْمَ مِنْ اَمْرِاللّٰهِ اِلَّا مَنْ رَّحِمَ

This points out that the deluge of carnal passions is similar to the deluge of Noah in its severity and danger. (*Barāhīn-e-Aḥmadiyyah*, vol. V, *Rūḥānī Khazā'in*, vol. 21, p. 205–206)

32. …Save that whereon my Lord has mercy. Yūsuf, 12:54
33. There is no shelter for *anyone* this day, from the decree of Allah, excepting those to whom He shows mercy. Hūd, 11:44

In summary, the carnal passions will always try to vanquish you. Avoid them, ever seeking the mercy of Allah. In these days, many other paths to it have been opened. Therefore, we need to pray and turn to Allah seeking His mercy more than ever before.[34]

اَلَا لِلّٰهِ الدِّيْنُ الْخَالِصُ. وَالَّذِيْنَ اتَّخَذُوْا مِنْ دُوْنِهٖ اَوْلِيَآءَ مَا نَعْبُدُهُمْ اِلَّا لِيُقَرِّبُوْنَآ اِلَى اللّٰهِ زُلْفٰى. اِنَّ اللّٰهَ يَحْكُمُ بَيْنَهُمْ فِىْ مَا هُمْ فِيْهِ يَخْتَلِفُوْنَ. اِنَّ اللّٰهَ لَا يَهْدِىْ مَنْ هُوَ كَاذِبٌ كَفَّارٌ

> Hearken, it is to Allah *alone* that sincere obedience is due. And those who take for protectors others beside Him *say*, 'We serve them only that they may bring us near to Allah in station.' Surely, Allah will judge between them concerning that wherein they differ. Surely, Allah guides not him who is an ungrateful liar.

The Promised Messiah[as] says:

> Believe in the God, Whose existence is confirmed unanimously by the Torah, the Gospels and the Holy Qur'ān. Do not fashion a god whose existence is not proven by the unanimous testimony of these three books. Accept that which is testified by intellect and human conscience and is testified by the books of God. Do not believe in God in a manner that creates discord between the books of God. Do not commit adultery. Do not tell lies. Avoid the evil look. Safeguard yourselves from wickedness and immorality, cruelty, dishonesty, and ways of rebellion. Do not be overpowered by carnal desires. Establish the five daily Prayers because human natures

34. Al-Zumar, 39:4

undergo five kinds of trials. Be grateful to your noble Messenger and invoke blessings upon him, for he is the one who showed you the way of recognising God in the age of darkness. These are the principles that are the distinguishing features of my Community. The way this Community establishes human sympathy, avoiding to do harm to human beings, and forsaking the opposition of the official in charge, are not found in other Muslims. Because of their own mistakes, their principles are of a different type, which do not need explanation at this time. (*Ḍamīmah Tiryāq-ul-Qulūb, Rūḥānī Khazā'in*, vol. 15, p. 524–526)

CONDITION III

That he/she shall regularly offer the five daily Prayers in accordance with the commandments of God and the Holy Prophet Muḥammad[sa] *and shall try his/her best to be regular in offering the tahajjud and invoking durūd on the Holy Prophet Muḥammad*[sa]*. That he/she shall make it his/her daily routine to ask forgiveness for his/her sins, to remember the bounties of God and to praise and glorify Him.*

Observe Five Daily Prayers

The first point mentioned in this condition is that the initiate will observe five daily Prayers in accordance with the commandment of Allah and His Messenger[sa]. The commandment of Allah is that men and women as well as children who have reached the age of ten should offer Prayers at their appointed times. Men have been commanded to establish five daily Prayers in congregation, to visit the mosques and inhabit them, and to search for the Grace of Allah. There is no concession in the matter of five daily Prayers. In cases of travel or sickness, some of the requirements have been made lenient, for instance combining Prayers or reducing the number of *rak'āt*. The fact that only during sickness one is permitted not to go to mosque to join Prayers shows the importance of Prayer in congregation.

I will read some excerpts, but I wish to stress that everyone who takes the pledge should ponder that whereas we are making a pledge to sell ourselves, are we obeying this explicit commandment of the Holy Qur'ān? Every Aḥmadī has the duty to remind himself. You should examine yourself, and watch your own actions. If we all start examining ourselves, a great revolution can be achieved.

In the Holy Qur'ān Allah says:[35]

وَاَقِيْمُوْا الصَّلٰوةَ وَاٰتُوْا الزَّكٰوةَ وَاَطِيْعُوْا الرَّسُوْلَ لَعَلَّكُمْ تُرْحَمُوْنَ

And observe Prayer and give the *Zakāt*, and obey the Messenger, that you may be shown mercy.

In *sūrah* Ṭā Hā, verse fifteen it is commanded:[36]

اِنَّنِىۡٓ اَنَا اللّٰهُ لَآ اِلٰهَ اِلَّآ اَنَا فَاعۡبُدۡنِىۡ وَاَقِمِ الصَّلٰوةَ لِذِكۡرِىۡ

'Verily, I am Allah; there is no God beside Me. So serve Me, and observe Prayer for My remembrance.'

35. Al-Nūr, 24:57
36. Ṭā Hā, 20:15

There are numerous other verses in the Holy Qur'ān about establishing Prayer. I will now present one *ḥadīth*.

> Ḥaḍrat Jābir[ra] relates that he heard the Holy Prophet[sa] say that, 'Neglecting to offer Prayer brings a man closer to apostasy and disbelief.' (*Ṣaḥīḥ Muslim*, Kitāb-ul-Īmān, Bābu Bayān-iṭlāq-ismil-Kufri 'Alā man Tarakaṣ-Ṣalāh)

The Holy Prophet[sa] has said, 'The comfort of my eye is in the Prayer.'

> Ḥaḍrat Abū Hurairah[ra] narrates that the Holy Prophet[sa] said, 'The first thing for which a person would be called to account is the Prayer. If he succeeds in this account, he would be successful and will attain salvation. If that account is deficient, he will be ruined and will be a loser. If there is a shortfall in the obligatory Prayers, Allah will make it up from his *nawāfil*. Similarly, all his other deeds will be accounted for.' (*Sunan-ut-Tirmadhī,* Kitāb-uṣ-Ṣalāti, Bābu Inna Awwala mā Yuḥāsabu bihil 'Abdu…)

Then it is said in a *ḥadīth*:

> Ḥaḍrat Abū Hurairah[ra] has related that he heard the Holy Prophet[sa] saying, 'Tell me if one of you had a stream running at his door and he should take a bath in it five times every day, would any dirt be left upon him?' He was answered, 'No dirt would be left on him.' The Holy Prophet[sa] observed, 'This is the case of the five Prayers. Allah wipes out all faults in consequence of them.' (*Ṣaḥīḥ Al-Bukhārī*, Kitābu Mawāqītiṣ-Ṣalāti, Bābuṣ-Ṣalātil Khamsi Kaffāratun Lil Khatā')

The Promised Messiah[as] says:

> Offer the Prayer. Offer the Prayer. That is the key to all good fortune. (*Izāla-e-'Auhām*, *Rūḥānī Khazā'in*, vol. 3, p. 549)

He also says:

> The essence and spirit of Prayer lie in supplications. (*Ayyām-uṣ-Ṣulḥ*, *Rūḥānī Khazā'in*, vol. 14, p. 241)

He also says:

> So all ye people who count yourselves as members of my Jamā'at, in heaven you shall be counted members of my following only when you truly begin to advance on the paths of righteousness. Offer your five daily Obligatory Prayers with such concentration and awe of mind as though you were seeing God in front of you. Observe the days of fasting for the sake of God in full sincerity. All among you who are liable for *Zakāt* should never fail to discharge this important obligation. And those upon whom the pilgrimage to Mecca has become obligatory, without any obstacles standing in the way, should duly undertake that blessed journey. Do all good deeds with the proper care they deserve, forsaking evil from a real repulsion arising from the heart. Be very sure that no action, whatsoever, can take you to God if it is devoid of righteousness. The root of everything good is *taqwā* [righteousness]; in whatever action this root is not lost, that action will never be devoid or futile. (*Kashti-e-Nūḥ*, *Rūḥānī Khazā'in*, vol. 19, p. 15)

The Promised Messiah[as] says:

> What is the Prayer? It is the supplication made humbly in the form of *tasbīh* [glorification] and *taḥmīd* [praise of God], *taqdīs* [proclaiming His holiness], *istighfār* [seeking His forgiveness] and *durūd* [calling down His blessings on the Holy Prophet[sa]]. When you are occupied with the Prayer, do not confine yourselves only to the prescribed Prayers like heedless people whose Prayer is all formality and has no reality behind it. When you observe the Prayer, besides the prescribed supplications taught by the Holy Qur'ān and the Holy Prophet[sa], you should set forth your supplications in your respective vernaculars so that your hearts may be moved by your humility and your earnestness. (*Kashti-e-Nūḥ, Rūḥānī Khazā'in*, vol. 19, p. 68–69)

The Promised Messiah[as] further says:

> The Prayer is so powerful that the heavens incline towards the human with it. The one who does full justice to Prayers feels that he has died; his soul has melted and fallen at the threshold of Allah... A house in which Prayer is offered in this manner will never face destruction. It is said in *ḥadīth* that if Prayer had been ordained to the people of Noah, they would not have been ruined. *Ḥajj* is obligatory but with certain prerequisites; so is fasting and *Zakāt*. But the obligation to offer Prayer has no prerequisites. All other obligations are discharged once a year, but the Prayer is ordained five times a day. As long as the Prayer is not performed in accordance with all its requirements, it does not earn the blessings that it carries.

Such allegiance [without discharging these obligations] in not of any benefit. (*Malfūẓāt*, new ed., vol. 3, p. 627)

The Promised Messiah[as] says:

Prayer is obligatory on every Muslim. It is narrated in *ḥadīth* that some people accepted Islām and submitted, 'O Prophet of Allah, please release us from the obligation of Prayer because we are traders. Because we tend to cattle, sometimes we are not sure about the cleanliness of our clothes. Moreover, we do not have the time.' The Holy Prophet[sa] said, 'Take heed, if there is no Prayer, there is nothing. Faith without worship is no faith at all.'

What is Prayer? To submit your weaknesses before God and to seek their solutions from Him. At times, to stand straight before him in awe of His Grandeur—ready to carry out His commands. At times, to prostrate before Him in complete submission. To beg from him all that you need. That is Prayer. To praise Him like a beggar, to move His Mercy by narrating His Greatness and Grandeur, and then asking. A 'faith' that does not have this [type of Prayer] is no faith at all.

A man is needy at all times to seek Allah's pleasure and beg for His Grace. Only through His Grace can we accomplish anything. O Allah, grant us the ability to belong entirely to You to stay firmly upon the path of Your pleasure and thereby earn Your pleasure. Prayer means love of God, fear of God, to always keep Him in mind—and that is what faith is.

So anyone who wants to be freed from the obligation of Prayer cannot accomplish anything more than the animals—

eating, drinking, and sleeping. This certainly is not faith. This is the way of the disbelievers. The popular saying, 'The moment of heedlessness is the moment of disbelief' is undoubtedly true and correct.' (*Tafsīr Ḥaḍrat Masīḥ-e-Mau'ūd*[as], new ed., vol. 3, p. 611–612, printed in Rabwah)

How to Achieve Concentration in Prayer? The Promised Messiah[as] says [that a person who derives no pleasure from Prayer should beg before Allah]:

"Allah! Thou knowest how blind and sightless I am, and at the moment I am like the dead. I know that in a little while I shall be called and shall present myself before Thee and no one will be able to stop me. But my heart is blind and unenlightened. Do Thou cause to descend upon it such a flame of light that thereby it may be inspired with Thy love and devotion. Do Thou bestow upon me such grace that I shall not be raised up sightless and blind."

When he supplicates in this manner and persists in the supplication, he will see that a time will arrive when something will descend upon him while he is engaged in such a Prayer that will melt his heart. (*Malfūẓāt*, new ed., vol. 2, p. 616)

Be Regular in Tahajjud

The third condition stipulates that one should offer *tahajjud* Prayers. Almighty Allah says:[37]

وَ مِنَ الَّيْلِ فَتَهَجَّدْ بِهٖ نَافِلَةً لَّكَ. عَسٰۤى اَنْ يَّبْعَثَكَ رَبُّكَ مَقَامًا مَّحْمُوْدًا

> And offer tahajjud with the recitation of the Qur'ān in a part of the night as a supererogatory service for thee. Very soon thy Lord will raise thee to an exalted station.

> Ḥaḍrat Bilāl[ra] narrates that the Holy Prophet[sa] said, 'You should be very regular in *tahajjud*. That has been the practice of the righteous ones in the past and is a means of attaining nearness to God. This is a habit that safeguards against sin, removes blemishes and safeguards from physical illness.' (*Sunan-ut-Tirmadhī*, Abwābud-Da'wāt)

In another *ḥadīth:*

> Ḥaḍrat Abū Hurairah[ra] has related that the Holy Prophet[sa] said, 'Our Lord descends every night to the lowest heaven. When one-third of the night remains, Allah says, "Who will call upon Me, so I should respond to him? Who will beg of Me, so I should grant him? And Who will ask my forgiveness, so I should forgive him?" Allah the Almighty keeps saying so until dawn breaks.' (*Musnadu Aḥmadabni Ḥanbal*, vol. 2, p. 521, printed in Beirut)

Many members of the Community write letters for prayers. If they practice this method of prayer themselves, they will see the blessings of Allah pouring upon them.

> Ḥaḍrat Abū Hurairah[ra] narrates that the Holy Prophet[sa] said, 'Allah the Almighty says that whoever is an enemy of My friend, I declare war on him. My servant can be close to Me through things that I love and that I have made obligatory

37. Banī Isrā'īl, 17:80

upon him. By offering *nawāfil* My servant gets so close to Me that I start loving him. When I make him a friend of Mine, I become the ears with which he hears, the eyes with which he sees, the hands with which he holds, and the feet with which he walks. That is, I fulfil all that he desires. If he begs of Me, I provide for him; if he seeks My protection, I grant him protection.' (*Ṣaḥīḥ Al-Bukhārī*, Kitāb-ur-Riqāqi, Bābut-Tawāḍu'i)

Ḥaḍrat Abū Hurairah[ra] has related that the Holy Prophet[sa] said, 'Allah will have mercy on a man who gets up at night for his [voluntary] Prayer and awakens his wife for the same purpose, and if she hesitates he sprinkles water over her face to wake her up. And, Allah will have mercy on a woman who gets up at night to offer [voluntary] Prayer and awakens her husband for the same purpose, and if he hesitates sprinkles water over his face to wake him up.' (*Sunano Abī Dāwūd*, Kitāb-uṣ-Ṣalāti)

The Promised Messiah[as] says:

Our Jamā'at should make it incumbent upon itself to offer *tahajjud*. Anyone who cannot do more should make at a minimum two *rak'āt* because he will get an opportunity to make some supplications. Supplications made at this time have a very special characteristic because they are offered with true pain and eagerness. Until there is a special pain and heartfelt agony, how can one wake up from comfortable sleep? To wake up at this time creates a heartfelt pain, which creates a condition of devotion and distress, which in turn become the means of acceptance of supplication. But someone who is lax in waking up is obviously lacking in pain and anguish. But one who wakes up, obviously there is a pain that is waking him up. (*Malfūzāt*, new ed., vol. 2, p. 182)

The Promised Messiah[as] also says:

Get up at night and supplicate that Allah the Almighty may guide you to His path. The companions of the Holy Prophet[sa] also received their training step by step. What were they before? They were like the a seed sown by a farmer. The Holy Prophet[sa] in turn watered and prayed for it. The seed was healthy, and the soil was fertile. With watering, it yielded excellent fruit. They walked the path of the Holy Prophet[sa] without hesitation. They did not wait for day or night. You should repent with a true heart. Wake up for *tahajjud*. Straighten your hearts. Leave your weaknesses, and make your words and deeds correspond to the will of Allah the Almighty. (*Malfūzāt*, new ed., vol. 1, p. 28)

Be Very Regular in Sending Durūd Upon the Holy Prophet Muḥammad[sa]

The third condition also requires that the initiate shall be ever eager to offer *durūd* upon the Holy Prophet[sa]. In this connection Almighty Allah says in the Holy Qur'ān:[38]

إِنَّ اللّٰهَ وَمَلٰٓئِكَتَهٗ يُصَلُّوْنَ عَلَى النَّبِيِّ يٰٓاَيُّهَا الَّذِيْنَ اٰمَنُوْا صَلُّوْا عَلَيْهِ وَسَلِّمُوْا تَسْلِيْمًا

38. Al-Aḥzāb, 33:57

> Allah and His angels send mercy on the Prophet. O ye who believe! You *also* should invoke blessings on him and salute *him* with abundant salutations of peace.

> Ḥaḍrat ‘Abdullāh Bin ‘Amr Bin al-‘Āṣ[ra] narrates that he heard the Holy Prophet[sa] saying, ‘When you hear the caller of *adhān*, repeat the words that he is saying. Then invoke Allah’s blessings upon me. He who invokes Allah’s blessing upon me, Allah will grant him His mercy ten-fold.’ Then he said, ‘Whoever begs Allah that He may grant me *waṣīlah*—which is one grade in Paradise, which Allah will grant to one of His servants, and I hope that I am that one—my intercession for such a one will become permissible.’ (*Ṣaḥīḥ Muslim*, Kitāb-uṣ-Ṣalāti, Bābul-Qauli mithli Qaulil Mua’dhdhini liman Sami‘ahū Thumma Yuṣallī ‘Alan Nabiyyi)

Everyone should keep in mind that in order to win the pleasure of Allah, to attain His love, and to have our prayers find acceptance with Allah, we need the intermediation of the Holy Prophet[sa]. The best way to do that—as we are told in the *ḥadīth*—is to invoke Allah’s blessings upon him. The Promised Messiah[as] has also admonished that *durūd* should be recited abundantly.[39]

اَللّٰهُمَّ صَلِّ عَلٰى مُحَمَّدٍ وَّعَلٰى آلِ مُحَمَّدٍ كَمَا صَلَّيْتَ عَلٰى اِبْرَاهِيْمَ
وَعَلٰى آلِ اِبْرَاهِيْمَ اِنَّكَ حَمِيْدٌ مَّجِيْدٌ ۔اَللّٰهُمَّ بَارِكْ عَلٰى مُحَمَّدٍ وَّعَلٰى
آلِ مُحَمَّدٍ كَمَا بَارَكْتَ عَلٰى اِبْرَاهِيْمَ وَعَلٰى آلِ اِبْرَاهِيْمَ اِنَّكَ حَمِيْدٌ
مَّجِيْدٌ۔

> Ḥaḍrat ‘Amīr Bin Rabī‘ah[ra] narrates that the Holy Prophet[sa] said, ‘A Muslim who invokes Allah’s blessings upon me will

continue to receive the blessings from the angels as long as he continues. Let him, if he wishes, shorten the time or prolong it.'

Ḥaḍrat 'Umar Bin al-Khaṭṭāb[ra] says, 'The supplication remains suspended between heaven and earth. Until someone invokes blessings upon the Holy Prophet[sa], no part of it goes up to be presented before Allah the Almighty.' (Sunan-ut-Tirmadhī, Kitāb-uṣ-Ṣalāti, Bābu mā jā'a fī Faḍliṣ-Ṣalāti 'Alan Nabiyyi)

Ḥaḍrat 'Abdullāh Bin Mas'ūd[ra] narrates that the Holy Prophet[sa] said, 'On the Day of Judgement, the closest to me will be those who invoke Allah's blessings upon me most frequently.' (Sunan-ut-Tirmadhī, Kitāb-uṣ-Ṣalāti, Bābu mā jā'a fī Faḍliṣ-Ṣalāti 'Alan Nabiyyi)

The Promised Messiah[as] narrates his personal experience as follows:

Once it so happened that I was completely absorbed in invoking Allah's blessing upon the Holy Prophet[sa] for a long period of time because I was certain that the paths of reaching Allah the Almighty are very narrow and cannot be found except through the intermediation of the Holy Prophet[sa]. As Allah also says:[40]

وَابْتَغُوْٓا اِلَيْهِ الْوَسِيْلَةَ

39. Bless O Allah, Muḥammad and his progeny as You did bless Abraham and his progeny. Certainly You are Praiseworthy and Glorious. Prosper O Allah, Muḥammad and his progeny, as You did prosper Abraham and his progeny. Certainly You are Praiseworthy and Glorious.

After a period of time I saw a vision that two water-men enter my house, one from the interior side and the other from the exterior. On their shoulders they were carrying waterskins filled with the light Divine. They said:[41]

هٰذا بِمَا صَلَّيْتَ عَلٰى مُحَمَّدٍ

(*Ḥaqīqat-ul-Waḥyi*, p. 128, footnote, *Rūḥānī Khazā'in*, vol. 22, p. 131, footnote)

Through invoking blessings upon the Holy Prophet[sa]... it is my personal experience that, Divine grace in the shape of wonderful light proceeds in the direction of the Holy Prophet[sa] and is absorbed into his bosom and then issuing therefrom numberless streams of it reach everyone deserving them according to his capacity. Certainly, no grace can reach anyone without the agency of the Holy Prophet[sa]. Invoking blessings on the Holy Prophet[sa] brings into movement his throne from which these streams of light issue. He who desires to obtain the grace of God Almighty should invoke blessings on him persistently, so that divine grace might be brought into motion. (*Al-Ḥakam*, February 28, 1903, p. 7)

The Promised Messiah[as] says:

Man is a servant or slave. A slave is one who carries out all commandments of the master. Similarly, if you want to achieve grace through the Holy Prophet[sa] it is essential that

---

40. ...and seek the way of approach unto Him... Al-Mā'idah, 5:36
41. This is a consequence of the blessings you invoked upon Muḥammad[sa].

you become his slave. Almighty Allah says in the Holy Qur'ān:[42]

قُلْ يٰعِبَادِىَ الَّذِيْنَ اَسْرَفُوْا عَلٰى اَنْفُسِهِمْ

Here, slave means an obedient servant and not a creation. To become a slave of the Holy Prophet[sa], it is essential to invoke Allah's blessings upon him, not to disobey any of his commandments and to carry out all his injunctions. (*Al-Badr*, vol. 2, No. 14, April 24, 1903, p. 109)

The Promised Messiah[as] says:

اَللّٰهُمَّ صَلِّ وَسَلِّمْ وَبَارِكْ عَلَيْهِ وَاٰلِهٖ بِعَدَدِ هَمِّهٖ وَ غَمِّهٖ وَ حُزْنِهٖ لِهٰذِهِ الْاُمَّةِ وَاَنْزِلْ عَلَيْهِ اَنْوَارَ رَحْمَتِكَ اِلَى الْاَبَدِ

(*Barakātud-Du'ā'*, *Rūḥānī Khazā'in*, vol. 6, p. 11)

Translation: O Allah send down blessings and peace on him and on his people proportionate to the amount of his suffering and sorrow for the sake of the *ummah* and send down upon him the light of Thy mercy forever.

Be Regular in Istighfār

The third condition also enjoins *istighfār*. Almighty Allah says in the Holy Qur'ān:[43]

فَقُلْتُ اسْتَغْفِرُوْا رَبَّكُمْ . اِنَّهٗ كَانَ غَفَّارًا . يُّرْسِلِ السَّمَآءَ عَلَيْكُمْ مِّدْرَارًا. وَّيُمْدِدْكُمْ بِاَمْوَالٍ وَّ بَنِيْنَ وَيَجْعَلْ لَّكُمْ جَنّٰتٍ وَّ يَجْعَلْ لَّكُمْ اَنْهٰرًا

42. Say, 'O My servants who have committed excesses against their own souls!…' Al-Zumar, 39:54

43. Al-Nūḥ, 11:13

'And I said, 'Seek forgiveness of your Lord; for He is the exceedingly Forgiving. He will send down clouds pouring rain for you in abundance, and He will strengthen you with wealth and *with* children, and He will give you gardens and He will give you rivers.

فَسَبِّحْ بِحَمْدِ رَبِّکَ وَاسْتَغْفِرْهُ. اِنَّهٗ كَانَ تَوَّابًا [44]

Glorify thy Lord with *His* praise and seek forgiveness of Him. Surely He is Oft-returning with *compassion*.

There is a *ḥadīth* on this subject.

Ḥaḍrat Abū Burdah Bin Abī Mūsā[ra] narrates from his father that the Holy Prophet[sa] said, 'Allah the Almighty has entrusted me with two trusts that I must convey to my *ummah* in the following verses of the Holy Qur'ān:[45]

وَمَا كَانَ اللّٰهُ لِيُعَذِّبَهُمْ وَاَنْتَ فِيْهِمْ. وَمَا كَانَ اللّٰهُ مُعَذِّبَهُمْ وَهُمْ يَسْتَغْفِرُوْنَ

But Allah would not punish them while thou wast among them, and Allah would not punish them while they sought forgiveness.

Therefore, when I leave them, I will leave *istighfār* with them up until the Day of Judgement.' (*Sunan-ut-Tirmadhī*, Kitābu Tafsīril-Qūr'ān. Tafsīru Sūratil-Anfāl)

Ḥaḍrat Ibn-e-'Abbās[ra] relates that the Holy Prophet[sa] said, 'Whoever clings to *istighfār* (i.e., performs it regularly and often) Allah the Almighty grants him a way out of all difficulties, and grants him ease under all difficulties, and grants him

44. Al-Naṣr, 110:4
45. Al-Anfāl, 8:34

provisions from ways that he could not imagine.' (*Sunano Abī Dāwūd*, Kitāb-ul-Witri, Bābun fil-Istighfār)

The Promised Messiah[as] says:

> ...*istighfār*, which brings strength upon the roots of faith, is mentioned in two ways in the Holy Qur'ān. One: to strengthen the love of Allah in one's heart, and through the relationship with Allah, stop the emergence of sins that arise in privacy—to be engrossed completely in God and to thereby seek His help. This is the *istighfār* of the elect, who consider it a ruin to be separated from Allah even for the briefest of the moments. They recite *istighfār* so that the mercy of Allah may keep sustaining them.
>
> The second type of *istighfār* is to emerge from the bondage of sin and to flee towards Allah; to try that, as a tree is firmly planted in the soil, your hearts should become completely devoted to Allah. Your hearts should thereby be captivated by the love of Allah and, by attaining pure nourishment, be saved from the dryness and decline of sin.
>
> These two types of *istighfār* have been called as such because *ghafara*, from which [the word] *istighfār* has been derived, means 'covering' or 'suppressing.' In other words, *istighfār* means that Allah may suppress the sins of someone who has immersed himself in His love and may not permit the roots of humanness from being exposed. Rather, He should grant him a place under the mantle of His Holiness; and if a root has been exposed because of any sin, He should cover it up again and save it from the ill-consequences of exposure.

Since Allah is the Source of all Grace, and His Light is ever-ready to remove all kinds of darkness, the only way of discovering the straight path is that we spread both arms towards this Fountain of Purity in fear of this dreadful condition so that the Fountain may move towards us with great force and should carry away all impurities. There is no greater sacrifice for pleasing Allah than to accept death for His sake and present ourselves before Him. (*Sirāj-ud-Dīn 'Īsā'ī ke Chār Swāloṅ kā Jawāb, Rūḥānī Khazā'in*, vol. 12, p. 346–347)

The Promised Messiah[as] also says:

> …When one seeks strength from Allah—that is, does *istighfār*—[one's] weaknesses can be removed with the help of the Holy Spirit and [one] can be safeguarded from sin like the Prophets and Messengers. And if there be someone who has already become a sinner, *istighfār* saves him from the consequences of his evil deeds, i.e., from punishment. For no darkness can stay in the face of light. But the wrong-doers who do not do *istighfār* suffer the consequences of their misdeeds. (*Kashti-e-Nūḥ, Rūḥānī Khazā'in*, vol. 19, p. 34)

The Promised Messiah[as] also says:

> Some people have an awareness of sin, others do not. Therefore, Almighty Allah has made *istighfār* incumbent for all times, so that one should continue to seek Allah's protection from all sins—obvious or hidden, known or unknown, whether

committed by hand, legs, tongue, nose, or eyes. These days the prayer of Ḥaḍrat Ādam[as] should especially be recited:[46]

رَبَّنَا ظَلَمْنَآ اَنْفُسَنَا وَ اِنْ لَّمْ تَغْفِرْلَنَا وَ تَرْحَمْنَا لَنَكُوْنَنَّ مِنَ الْخَاسِرِيْن

This prayer has already been accepted. Do not spend your life in heedlessness. Anyone who eschews heedless life will hopefully never be afflicted with any great misfortune because such misfortune does not befall without Divine permission. I was revealed the following prayer in this regard:[47]

رَبِّ كُلُّ شَيْءٍ خَادِمُكَ رَبِّ فَاحْفَظْنِيْ وَانْصُرْنِيْ وَارْحَمْنِيْ

(*Malfūẓāt*, new ed., vol. 2. p. 577)

Istighfār and Repentance

The Promised Messiah[as] says:[48]

وَ اَنِ اسْتَغْفِرُوْا رَبَّكُمْ ثُمَّ تُوْبُوْا اِلَيْهِ

Remember, the Muslims have been bestowed two thing—one for obtaining strength and the other for the practical demonstration of the strength that has been obtained. *Istighfār* is for obtaining strength. It is also called seeking help. The *ṣūfis* have said that as physical strength and power are fostered through

46. …'Our Lord we have wronged ourselves; and if Thou forgive us not and have not mercy on us, we shall surely be of the lost.' Al-A'rāf, 7:24
47. O my Lord, everything is in your service. O My Lord, protect me, and help me, and have mercy on me.
48. And that you seek forgiveness of your Lord, *and* then turn to Him.… Hūd, 11:4

exercise, in the same way *istighfār* is spiritual exercise. Through it, the soul obtains strength and the heart achieves steadfastness. He who desires strength should do *istighfār.*

Ghafara literally means covering and suppressing. With *istighfār,* man tries to suppress and cover [those] emotions that keep him away from God. Thus, the only meaning of *istighfār* is that the poisonous elements that may well-nigh destroy a man may be overpowered, and one should give practical shape to the commandment of God by avoiding all obstructions.

Remember that Almighty Allah has created two types of elements within human beings. One: the poisonous element, which is activated by Satan. Second: the remedial element. When someone is proud and considers himself to be worth something, and does not seek help from the remedial fountain, the poisonous element gains the upper hand. But when he considers himself unworthy and insignificant and feels within him the need for Divine help, Allah creates a fountain for him that makes his soul flow. This is the meaning of *istighfār,* namely, to find this strength to overpower the poisonous element. (*Malfūzāt,* new ed., vol. 1, p. 348–349, printed in Rabwah)

Always Express Gratitude to Allah

The third condition also includes an injunction to remain ever-thankful to Allah. In this respect Allah the Almighty says in the Holy Qur'ān:

اَلْحَمْدُلِلّٰهِ رَبِّ الْعٰلَمِيْنَ [49]

All praise belongs to Allah, Lord of all the worlds.

اَلْحَمْدُ لِلّٰهِ الَّذِىْ لَهٗ مَا فِى السَّمٰوٰتِ وَمَا فِى الْاَرْضِ وَ لَهُ
الْحَمْدُ فِى الْاٰخِرَةِ. وَهُوَ الْحَكِيْمُ الْخَبِيْرُ [50]

All praise is due to Allah, to Whom belongs whatever is in the heavens and whatever is in the earth. And His is all praise in the Hereafter; and He is the Wise, the All-Aware.

Ḥaḍrat Abū Hurairah[ra] has related that the Holy Prophet[sa] said, 'Every matter of importance that is not begun with the praise of Allah remains defective.' Another version is: 'Every speech that is not begun with the praise of Allah is devoid of blessings.' (*Sunano Ibn-e-Mājah*, Kitāb-ul-Jihād, Abwābun-Nikāḥ.Also *Sunano Abī Dāwūd*, Kitāb-ul-Adab)

There is another *ḥadīth:*

Ḥaḍrat No'mān Bin Bashīr[ra] narrates that the Holy Prophet[sa] said from his pulpit, 'He who is not grateful for small favours cannot be grateful for the bigger ones. He who cannot be thankful to men cannot render thanks for the favours of Allah. To talk about the blessings of Allah the Almighty is thankfulness; to not mention them is ingratitude.' (*Musnadu Aḥmadabni Ḥanbal*, vol. 4, p. 278, printed in Beirut)

Ḥaḍrat Mu'ādh[ra] has related that the Holy Prophet[sa] held him by his hand and said, 'Mu'adh, I swear in the name of Allah! I

49. Al-Fātiḥah, 1:2
50. Saba', 34:2

do love you and counsel you that you should not miss supplicating after every *Ṣalāt*.

اَللّٰهُمَّ اَعِنِّیْ عَلٰی ذِکْرِکَ وَ شُکْرِکَ وَحُسْنِ عِبَادَتِکَ

Allah, help me in remembering You, and being grateful to You and worshipping You in the best manner.' (*Sunano Abī Dāwūd*, Kitāb-ul-Witri, Bābun fil-Istighfār)

The Promised Messiah[as] says:

> If someone ponders deeply, he would realise that all praises and good attributes belong to Allah the Almighty alone. No human or other creature deserves true praise and appreciation. If one were to reflect without any tinge of selfishness, one would obviously discover that one who creates something, at a time when it did not exist nor was there any information about its existence, such a one should be worthy of praise. And [such a one should also be worthy of praise] who created necessary means at a time when nothing existed, nor was there any information available about the basic requirement for creation, sustenance, good health, and maintenance of existence. And [such a one should also be worthy of praise] who had mercy on a creature that suffered great misfortune and who had relieved it from that misfortune. And [such a one should also be worthy of praise] who does not let the efforts of a hard worker go to waste and gives full reward to those who make the effort. Eventhough payment of due wages is a right of the labourer, someone who makes due payment can also be a benefactor. All of these are excellent traits that can make one worthy of praise and appreciation.

Now, ponder and you will recognise that all the praiseworthy attributes belong to Allah alone because He alone possesses all these attributes in perfection; and nobody else does.... In short, only Allah the Almighty is perfect in His being and worthy of praise in an excellent manner. In comparison to Him, no one deserves praise by virtue of its own being. If someone else deserves praise, it is only secondary in nature. This, too, is a Mercy of Allah the Almighty because eventhough He is One, without any partner, He has included others in those praises in a secondary sense. (*Ro'idād-e-Jalsah Du'ā'*, *Rūḥānī Khazā'in*, vol. 15, p. 598–602)

Giving a general admonition to the Jamā'at, the Promised Messiah[as] says:

If you desire that the angels should praise you in heaven, then endure beating and be joyful, hear abuse and be grateful, experience failure and do not cut asunder your relationship with God. You are the last Jamā'at of God, so practice virtue at its highest level. Anyone from among you who becomes slothful will be cast out of the Jamā'at like a foul thing and will die in sorrow without having caused any harm to God. I give you the good news that your God truly exists. All are His creatures, but He chooses the one who chooses Him. He comes to the one who goes to Him. He bestows honour upon the one who honours Him. So approach Him with straight hearts and pure tongues, eyes and ears so that He may accept you. (*Kashti-e-Nūḥ, Rūḥānī Khazā'in*, vol. 19, p. 15)

The Promised Messiah[as] also says:

> Don't think that God will let you go to waste. You are a seed of the Hand of God which was sown in the earth. God says that this seed will grow and flower and its branches will spread in all directions and it will become a huge tree. So blessed is he who believes in what God says and does not fear the trials that he suffers on his way to God. For the coming of trials is essential so that God may try you to see who is true in his declaration of *bai'at* and who is false. Whoever slips at a trial, he would do no harm to God whatsoever and ill-luck would take him to hell. Were he not born, it would have been better for him. But all those who remain steadfast till the end—they will be shaken with quakes of calamities, and storms of misfortune will batter them, people will jeer and mock them, and the world will treat them with extreme hatred—shall at last come out victorious. And doors of blessings shall be opened to them. God addressed me and said that I should inform my Jamā'at that those who believe and their belief is not adulterated with worldly considerations and is free from hypocrisy and cowardice and is such as it does not fall short of any stage of obedience, these are the people who are favourites of God. And God says that these are the very people who have a sure footing with their Lord. (*Al-Waṣiyyat, Rūḥānī Khazā'in*, vol. 20, p. 309)

May Allah the Almighty enable all of us to hold fast to these admonitions. May He make us true Aḥmadīs and grant us the ability to be always true to our pledge of allegiance. May He make us truly obedient to Allah the Almighty and His

Apostle. May we never commit anything that blemishes the lovely Jamā'at of the Promised Messiah[as].

O Allah! Forgive our mistakes, conceal our shortcomings, count us always among those who are obedient and faithful to You. Make us hold fast to the pledge of allegiance. Include us among those whom You love. Enable our future generations also to remain true to the pledge. May we never distance ourselves from You. Grant us Your true recognition. O Most Merciful of all mercifuls, have mercy upon us. Accept all our supplications. Make us the inheritors of all the prayers that the Promised Messiah[as] made for those who join his Jamā'at.

[From the concluding address delivered at the Annual Convention of the Aḥmadiyyah Muslim Jamā'at, Germany, on August 24, 2003, in which fourth, fifth and sixth conditions of bai'at were explained in detail.]

...This is a very important subject and its need is felt in this age even more. As we move away from the period of the Promised Messiah[as], we are prone to feel proud of belonging to the lineage of a particular Companion[ra] of the Promised Messiah[as], yet we are often not as conscious of the sacrifices rendered by our forefathers as we should be. And, though we have inherited their genes, the standards of spirituality have declined. While it is a natural phenomenon that as we move away from the period of Prophethood, some shortcomings and weaknesses may occur, it is important to note that progressive communities do not rest assured by simply blaming the new conditions of changed times as the root of this ill. On the contrary, they keep striving, trusting in the glad tidings and prophecies as members of the Jamā'at of the Promised Messiah and the Mahdī[as]. It is they who will educate the world in the teachings of the Holy Prophet Muḥammad[sa]. The condition set forth for us to achieve this goal is that we should stand firm in the belief of the Oneness of God, not only for ourselves but that we should strive to make our next generations stand firm in this belief as well. Now I will present to you an excerpt from the writings of the

Promised Messiah[as] to clarify what he expected of those who took his covenant of *bai'at*...

The Promised Messiah[as] say:

> Seeking forgiveness at my hands demands a type of a death so that you may be given birth to a new life. It is purposeless to take the pledge of *bai'at* without sincerity of heart. When you take my pledge of *bai'at*, God expects an undertaking from your heart. So the one who accepts me with a true heart and truly seeks forgiveness of his sins, the Forgiving and Merciful God surely forgives his sins. Thus he becomes like a person like one just born of his mother; then the angels protect him. (*Malfūẓāt,* vol. 3, p. 262)

CONDITION IV

That under the impulse of any passions, he/she shall cause no harm whatsoever to the creatures of God in general and Muslims in particular, neither by his/her tongue, hands, nor any other means.

As is clear from this condition, one should not cause harm whether by one's hands or by one's tongue in a fit of anger, under the pretext of one's self-respect or honour. Clearly, it is mandatory that one should not harm any Muslim. This has been made obligatory upon us. We have to especially abide by this condition because Muslims associate themselves with our dearly Beloved Master the Holy Prophet Muḥammad[sa]. We cannot even imagine harming them. In seeking the help of Allah, the Most Powerful and the Almighty God, Who is the Lord of All Powers, against those self-appointed *'ulema* who are a blemish on the fair name of Islām—who have exceeded all bounds in their enmity of the Messiah and the Mahdī[as] of the age—we prostrate at His threshold imploring Him to seize them. We do so because the

Prophet of Allah had declared them to be the worst of the creation; otherwise, we neither nurse unnecessary grudges against them nor are we angry with anyone. We act upon the commandments of the Almighty Allah. In exhorting us to suppress our anger the Almighty Allah says:[51]

اَلَّـذِيْـنَ يُـنْـفِقُوْنَ فِى السَّرَّآءِ وَالضَّرَّآءِ وَالْكَاظِمِيْنَ الْغَيْظَ وَالْعَافِيْنَ
عَنِ النَّاسِ وَاللّٰهُ يُحِبُّ الْمُحْسِنِيْنَ

> Those who spend in prosperity and in adversity, and those who suppress anger and pardon men; and Allah loves those who do good.

It was by virtue of this verse that a slave of Ḥaḍrat Imām Ḥusain[ra], won his freedom. It is said that the slave erroneously dropped something hot (it could have been water) on Ḥaḍrat Ḥusain[ra]. He looked at him angrily. The slave was intelligent and knew the Holy Qur'ān as well. He promptly quoted the part of the verse about the suppression of anger.[52]

وَالْكَاظِمِيْنَ الْغَيْظ

Ḥaḍrat Ḥusain[ra] said, 'You are right; I suppress my anger.' Now the servant thought that though the anger had been brought under control, it would still remain in his heart. It was possible that he would be chastised for some other mistake later. So he quoted the second part of the verse:[53]

وَالْـعَـافِيْنَ عَنِ النَّاس

---

51. Āl-e-'Imrān, 3:135
52. and those who suppress anger... Āl-e-'Imrān, 3:135

Ḥaḍrat Ḥusain said, 'I have forgiven you.' The slave's knowledge and promptness gave him immediate benefits. Now he quoted the third part of the verse:[54]

وَاللّٰهُ يُحِبُّ الْمُحْسِنِيْنَ

Ḥaḍrat Ḥusain responded, 'I hereby grant you freedom.' In those days, slaves used to be bought. It was not possible to gain one's freedom so easily. The slave's quick-wittedness and knowledge got him freedom from his master who was God-fearing. This is the teaching of Islām.

Adopt Forgiveness and Forbearance

With regard to moral qualities that relate to the attainment of virtue, the Promised Messiah[as] says:

> Of these, the first moral quality is forgiveness, that is, to forgive someone's sins. The virtue in this is that the person who commits a sin causes harm to someone else and, therefore, becomes liable to be punished or to be put in jail or to be fined or be chastised with direct action. Thus, to forgive him, if forgiveness is appropriate, would be a good deed. In this connection the teaching of the Holy Qur'ān is:

وَالْكَاظِمِيْنَ الْغَيْظَ وَالْعَافِيْنَ عَنِ النَّاسِ[55]

جَزَآءُ سَيِّئَةٍ سَيِّئَةٌ مِّثْلُهَا فَمَنْ عَفَا وَاَصْلَحَ فَاَجْرُهٗ عَلَى اللّٰهِ[56]

53. …and pardon men… Āl-e-'Imrān, 3:135
54. …and Allah loves those who do good. Āl-e-'Imrān, 3:135
55. Āl-e-'Imrān, 3:135
56. Al-Shur'āra', 26:41

That is, the virtuous are those who suppress their anger when it is appropriate and forgive when it is appropriate to forgive sins. (Āl-e-'Imrān, 3:135)

A bad deed should be requited with an equal amount and in situations where forgiveness of sin is corrective without causing any harm—that is, forgiveness is granted when the occasion warrants and not otherwise—then it merits reward. (*Islāmī Uṣūl kī Philosophy, Rūḥānī Khazā'in*, vol. 10, p. 351)

There is a famous tradition of the Holy Prophet[sa] that many have heard. Pointing towards his chest, the Holy Prophet[sa] said: '*Taqwā* lies in here.' That is to say, that pure and matchless *taqwā*, if it were to be found anywhere, lived only in the heart of the Holy Prophet[sa]. Besides *taqwā* there is nothing else in his heart.

So, O people, O community of believers, for you the everlasting instruction is that the example you have to emulate is the model of the Holy Prophet[sa]. So, search your hearts. Are you making efforts at imbuing yourselves with *taqwā* by emulating the example of the Holy Prophet[sa]? Do you also have the fear of Allah, and is His love in yourselves? As a result, do you have sympathy for and do you do good towards his Creation?

Now I place before you the tradition in full:

Ḥaḍrat Abū Hurairah[ra] narrates that the Holy Prophet[sa] said: 'Do not be jealous of one another. Do not quarrel among yourselves. Do not entertain malice against each other. Do not have enmities against one another. None of you should overbid on a contract that has been settled by the other. O servants of Allah, be brothers to one another. A Muslim is a brother to another Muslim. He does not oppress his brother. He does not derogate him nor thinks low of him.' Then pointing towards his chest the Holy Prophet[sa] said three times, '*Taqwā* is in here. It is enough evil for a man to think low of his brother. The blood, property and honour of every Muslim are unlawful for another Muslim.' (*Ṣaḥīḥ Muslim,* Kitāb-ul-Birri waṣ-Ṣilah, Bābu Taḥrīmī-Ẓulmil Muslimī Wa Khadhlih)

Do Not Cause Harm to Anyone

It has been stated in the fourth condition that one should not cause harm to another person whether by one's hand or one's tongue or through any other means. I will now explain this condition of *bai'at*. From the saying of the Holy Prophet[sa] that I have just presented before, you should focus on the words 'do not be jealous.' Jealousy ultimately develops into enmity. A person who has jealousy in his heart always wants to harm the person of whom he is jealous. Jealousy is a type of disease that while it causes harm to the other person, it also consumes the person who is jealous. It gives rise to many other petty feelings of spite, such as: why the other person has a better business, or more wealth or more talented children. In the case of women, jealousy may arise because of someone's better jewellery. Even in religious matters—where good deeds must be appreciated and where people should try to move forward in rendering service to the religion—efforts are made to place obstacles in the way of those who are rendering religious service by making accusations against them so that they, too, are deprived of performing service to the religion.

Then the Holy Prophet[sa] admonishes us not to quarrel with each other. Quarrels take place over petty matters. To give an example, sometimes an officer on duty warns a child who has been mischievous in a gathering that if he were to do it again he would be dealt with firmly or be corrected. The parents, sitting nearby, immediately roll up their sleeves for a fight, and the person performing the duty is put down in a terrible way. Through this action of theirs, they not only broke a condition of *bai'at* and spoiled their good manners, they also banished from the minds of their next generation the respect for the organisation of the Jamā'at and the distinction between good and bad.

Then we are directed not to have enmity towards each other. Enmities start from petty matters. Hearts are filled with spite and malice. Some people are always on the lookout for an opportunity to avenge them, while the instruction is not to have enmity with, nor malice for, anyone. Once a Companion[ra] humbly asked the Holy Prophet[sa] to give him simple, but unforgettable advice in a few words. The Holy Prophet[sa] advised him to 'shun anger' and then again he said, 'shun anger.' When you keep in your mind that you should shun anger, then malice and spite will go away automatically.

Another habit of 'injuring or harming someone, or making another person's deal go sour' is to overbid on a contract concluded by the other. In this saying, we have been asked to desist from such actions. A higher price is offered to acquire a thing only to bring the other person's business down while no personal gain is achieved from such a bid. This also applies to proposals for marriage. Aḥmadīs should keep that prohibition in mind.

Then the admonishment is not to oppress anyone, not to think low of anyone, nor to derogate anyone. An oppressor never achieves nearness to Allah. Then, how is it possible that on the one hand one would enter into a pledge of allegiance with the one appointed by Allah to win His favour and on the other one would oppress people by snatching their rights. It is a common practice in our villages not to give brothers their rights, not to give sisters their share of inheritance simply because they have been married to a different family, lest the property move out of the family, There are those that oppress their wives, those that do not respect their rights, and there are wives who do not respect the rights of their husbands. There are many such matters that fall under this category. Many such actions are indicative of the low treatment of others. While you claim to have taken *bai'at* and you claim to give up these evil deeds, how can you commit these actions? The clear-cut commandment is that it is not permissible for a Muslim to think poorly of another Muslim under any circumstances. Similarly, the blood, property and honour of a Muslim are made unlawful for another Muslim. So, having accepted the Appointed One of this age, you who act upon Islāmic teachings the most, how can these deeds be tolerated on your part, and how can you still be considered a member of the Jamā'at of the Promised Messiah[as]?

I would now present to you some *aḥādīth* that illustrate what the Companions[ra] of the Holy Prophet[sa] did in not taking these matters lightly and what changes they made in themselves after they had accepted Islām.

> Ḥaḍrat Abū Dhar al-Ghaffārī[ra] used to provide drinking water from his tank. Some members of a family came by. One of them asked the others as to which of them would go to Abū Dhar[ra] to hold him by his hair and ask him to render an account of himself. One of them said that he would do it. He went over to Abū Dhar[ra] when he was standing near the tank. He started questioning him. Abū Dhar[ra], who was standing at this time, sat down and then he lay down. One of them asked him, 'Abū Dhar[ra], why did you sit down and then why did you lie down?' He replied that, 'the Holy Prophet[sa] told us, "When anger overcomes one of you while he is standing he should sit down so that this anger would subside; failing that, he should lie down."' (*Musnadu Aḥmadabni Ḥanbal*, vol. 5, p. 153, printed in Beirut)

In another *ḥadīth* the narrator states that:

> We were sitting in the company of 'Urwah Bin Muḥammad when a man came by. He started talking in a manner that angered 'Urwah Bin Muḥammad. The narrator states that when his anger boiled he got up. After performing ablution, he came back to them. He told us that he had heard of a narration passed down by his father through his grandfather, 'Atiyyah, who was a Companion of the Holy Prophet[sa] that the Holy Prophet[sa] had said that anger comes from Satan. Satan was made from the fire, and fire is put out by water; so when one of you gets angry, he should perform the ablution. (*Musnadu Aḥmadabni Ḥanbal*, vol. 4, p. 226, printed in Beirut)
>
> Ḥaḍrat Ziyād[ra], on the basis of a narration provided by his uncle Ḥaḍrat 'Utbah[ra] used to supplicate, 'O my Allah, I seek

thy refuge from bad morals, evil deeds and evil desires.' (*Sunan-ut-Tirmadhī*, Abwābud-Da'wāt, Bābu Jāmi'id-Da'wāt)

I now present before you what the Promised Messiah[as] said in this regard and what he expects of the members of the Jamā'at.

The Promised Messiah[as] says:

> The members of my Jamā'at, wherever they might be, should listen with attention. The purpose of their joining this Movement and establishing the mutual relationship of spiritual preceptor and disciple with me is that they should achieve a high degree of good conduct, good behaviour and righteousness. No wrongdoing, mischief, or misconduct should even approach them. They should perform the five daily Prayers regularly, should not utter a falsehood and should not hurt anyone with their speech. They should be guilty of no vice and should not let even a thought of any mischief, or wrong, or disorderliness, or turmoil pass through their minds. They should shun every type of sin, offence, undesirable action, passion, and unmannerly behaviour. They should become pure-hearted and meek servants of God Almighty, and no poisonous germ should flourish in their beings.... Sympathy with mankind should be their principle and, they should fear God Almighty. They should safeguard their tongues and their hands and their thoughts against every kind of impurity, disorderliness and dishonesty. They should join the five daily Prayer services without fail. They should refrain from every kind of wrong, transgression, dishonesty, bribery, trespass, and partiality. They should not participate in any evil company. If it should be proved that one who frequents their company

does not obey God's commandments… or is not mindful of the rights of people, or is cruel or mischievous, or is ill-behaved, or is seeking to deceive the servants of God Almighty by speaking ill or abusively of them, or is guilty of imposture towards the persons with whom they have entered into a covenant of *bai'at*, it should be their duty to repel him and to keep away from such a dangerous one. They should not design harm against the followers of any religion or the members of any tribe or group. Be true well-wishers of everyone, and take care that no mischievous, vicious, disorderly, or ill-behaved person, should be ever of your company, or should dwell among you; for such a person could at any time be the cause of your stumbling.…

These are matters and conditions that I have been urging from the beginning, and it is the duty of every member of my Jamā'at to act upon them. You should indulge in no impurity, mockery or derision. Walk upon the earth with good hearts, pure tempers, and pure thoughts. Not every evil is worth fighting, so cultivate the habit of forgiveness and overlooking defaults, and behave with steadfastness and meekness. Do not attack anyone improperly, and keep your passions under complete control. If you take part in a discussion, or in an exchange of views on a religious subject, express yourself gently and be courteous. If anyone misbehaves towards you, withdraw from such company with a greeting of peace. If you are persecuted or reviled, be mindful that you should not meet stupidity with stupidity, for otherwise you will be counted in the same category as your opponents. God Almighty desires that you should become a *jamā'at* that should set an example of goodness and truthfulness for the whole world. Hasten to exclude everyone from your company who sets an example of evil, mischief, provocation and ill-behaviour. He who cannot dwell among us in meekness, goodness and piety, using gentle words and comporting himself in ways of good conduct, should depart from us quickly, for God does not desire that such a one should dwell among us. He will die miserably, for he did not adopt the way of goodness. Therefore, be alert, and be truly good-hearted, gentle and righteous. You will be recognised by your regular attendance at Prayer services and your high moral qualities. He who has the seed of evil embedded in him will not be able to conform to this admonition. (*Tablīgh-e-Risālat*, vol. 7, p. 42–43. *Ishtihār*, May 29, 1898)

He further said:

A man should not be conceited, nor indecent, nor ill-mannered towards the fellow beings. He should act with love and goodness and should not bear ill-will towards anyone for personal reasons. He should behave firmly or gently in accordance with the occasions or conditions. (*Malfūẓāt*, new ed., vol. 5, p. 609)

Adopt Meekness and Humility

With respect to meekness and humility the Promised Messiah[as] says:

...Seek forgiveness of Allah before the punishment of God comes to close the door of forgiveness. While the laws of this world are feared, why is it the laws of God are not? When calamities have occurred one has to go through them. Everyone should try to get up for *tahajjud* and to include *qunūt*[57] in the five daily Prayers as well. Repent from everything that would incur the wrath of Allah. Repentance means giving up all evil deeds and everything that goes against the pleasure of God and undergoing a true change and making progress and adopting the way of righteousness. In this, too, lies the mercy of Allah. Make your habits decent. Shun anger, replacing it with gentleness and meekness. Along with adopting good morals you should give charity as well.[58]

يُطْعِمُوْنَ الطَّعَامَ عَلٰى حُبِّهٖ مِسْكِيْناً وَّيَتِيْماً وَّاَسِيْرًا

Which means that for seeking the pleasure of God you feed the poor, the orphans, and the needy, and you say that you perform these acts only for the pleasure of the Almighty Allah, and you fear that extremely terrible Day.

In brief, pray, ask forgiveness and keep giving charity, so that the Almighty Allah may deal with you with His Grace and Mercy. (*Malfūẓāt,* new ed., vol. 1, p. 134–135)

Then he says:

Friends! Hold fast to this rule: deal with all people with kindness. Kindness increases intelligence, and forbearance promotes deeper thinking. Anyone who does not adopt this way is not of us. Anyone from our Jamā'at who cannot tolerate the abuse and harshness of our opponents is

57. A supplication for help and forgiveness of Allah made in *witr* Prayer.
58. Al-Dahr, 76:9

permitted to have recourse to the courts, but it is not appropriate that he should counter harshness with harshness and create a dispute. This is the admonishment we have given our Jamā'at, and we express our displeasure and declare that the one who does not act upon it is not of our Jamā'at. (*Tablīgh-e-Risālat*, vol. 6. p. 170)

CONDITION V

That he/she shall remain faithful to God in all circumstances of life, in sorrow and in happiness, in adversity and in prosperity, in felicity and in trial; and that he/she shall in all conditions remain resigned to the decree of God and keep himself/herself ready to face all kinds of indignities and sufferings in His way and shall never turn away from Him at the onslaught of any misfortune; on the contrary, he/she shall march forward.

Allah the Almighty says in the Holy Qur'ān:[59]

وَمِنَ النَّاسِ مَنْ يَّشْرِىْ نَفْسَهُ ابْتِغَآءَ مَرْضَاتِ اللّٰهِ وَاللّٰهُ رَءُوْفٌ بِالْعِبَادِ

And of men there is he who would sell himself to seek the pleasure of Allah; and Allah is Compassionate to *His* servants.

59. Al-Baqarah, 2:208

In explaining this verse of the Holy Qur'ān, the Promised Messiah[as] says:

> The people of the highest grade among the people—that is, people who are completely lost in the pleasure of Allah, and sell their selves to earn the pleasure of God—are the people upon whom the mercy of Allah descends.... In this verse Allah the Almighty says, 'Only he is delivered from all tribulations who sells his self in My way and for My pleasure. He proves with his utmost endeavours that he belongs to God and considers his entire being as something that has been fashioned for obedience of the Creator and service to the creation...' (*Report Jalsah A'zam Madhāhib*, p. 131–132)

Then he says:

> A loved one of God sells his being in the way of God. In return, he earns the pleasure of God. Such are the ones upon whom the special mercy of God descends. (*Report Jalsah A'zam Madhāhib*, p. 188)

Then he says:

> There are some people who sell their beings hoping that He would be pleased... (*Paighāmi Ṣulḥ, Rūḥānī Khazā'in*, vol. 23, p. 473)

For such people, Allah the Almighty has given the glad tiding:[60]

يٰٓأَيَّتُهَا النَّفْسُ الْمُطْمَئِنَّةُ. ارْجِعِىْ إِلٰى رَبِّكِ رَاضِيَةً مَّرْضِيَّةً
فَادْخُلِىْ فِىْ عِبَادِىْ. وَ ادْخُلِىْ جَنَّتِىْ.

> *And* thou, O soul at peace! Return to thy Lord well pleased *with Him and* He well pleased *with thee.* So enter thou among My servants. And enter thou My Garden.

People who are reconciled to the will of Allah, and suffer all hardships and tribulations for His sake, are never left unrewarded by Allah the Almighty. There are many among us who are embodiments of shortcomings and defects. We commit many errors and sins. But if we are in the habit of reconciling to the will of Allah, and are ever-prepared to, and do, suffer all indignities for Him, if we are not like the wailing woman who put up a big clamour on any small suffering, for such patient ones there is a glad tiding from the Holy Prophet[sa].

Sufferings of a Muslim Are an Expiation for Sins

> Ḥaḍrat Abū Hurairah[ra] narrates that the Holy Prophet[sa] said, 'No Muslim suffers any calamity, suffering, pain, discomfort, or anxiety, even as small as the prick of a thorn, but Allah wipes out instead some of his defaults and his sins.' (*Ṣaḥīḥ Muslim,* Kitāb-ul-Birri waṣ-Ṣilah, Bābu Thawābil-Mo'mini fī mā yuṣībuhū min Maraḍin au Ḥuznin)

In another *ḥadīth* Ḥaḍrat Ṣuhaib Bin Sinān[ra] has related that:

> The Holy Prophet[sa] said, 'Wondrous is the case of a believer; there is good for him in everything, and it is so for him alone. If he experiences something agreeable, he is grateful to God

60. Al-Fajr, 89:28–31.

> and that is good for him; and if he experiences adversity, he is steadfast and that is good for him because he earns merit for his steadfastness.' (*Ṣaḥīḥ Muslim,* Kitāb-uz-Zuhdi, Bābul Mo'mini Amruhū kulluhū Khair)

Sometimes Allah makes His servants go through sufferings related to his children. There is excessive wailing and crying at the death of children, especially among the women. Thanks to Allah, He has granted to the Aḥmadiyyah Muslim Jamā'at mothers who are very patient and reconciled to His will. But sometimes there are instances of complaining, especially among the illiterates or those with meagre education. In fact, I have also observed some cases among those with good education that they utter words of ingratitude.

There is a *ḥadīth* that the Holy Prophet[sa] used to take a pledge from women-Companions[ra] in this respect. The *ḥadīth* runs as follows:

> Ḥaḍrat Usaid[ra] relates that he heard from a woman-Companion[ra] who had taken a pledge at the hand of the Holy Prophet[sa] that the pledge included the following: 'We will not disobey the Holy Prophet[sa], will not tear our faces in wailing, will not raise a hue and cry during mourning, and will not tear our clothes or keep our hair ruffled.' (*Sunano Abī Dāwūd,* Kitāb-ul-Janā'iz, Bābun fin-Nūḥ)

Real Time to Show Patience is When the Tragedy Strikes

> Ḥaḍrat Anas[ra] relates that the Holy Prophet[sa] passed by a woman who was crying by the side of a grave. He said to her,

'Be mindful of thy duty to Allah and be steadfast.' She retorted, 'Leave me alone; you have not been afflicted as I have been.' She had not known who he was. Someone told her, 'That was the Holy Prophet[sa].' She proceeded to the door of the Holy Prophet[sa] and not finding any doorman went in and said to him, 'I had not recognised you.' He said, 'Steadfastness means to be resigned at the time of the first shock of grief.' (*Ṣaḥīḥ Al-Bukhārī*, Kitāb-ul-Janā'iz, Bābu Ziyāratil-Qubūr)

Another important point that has been emphasised in the fifth condition is [to remain steadfast] no matter how hard the circumstances, how long the period of hardship, how apparent the worldly attractions, how likely the benefits from diverse worldly activities, and how luring the attractions offered by the worldly powers that tells you not to worry because: 'as an Aḥmadī, even as you maintain ties to the Jamā'at, you can still conduct your professional affairs, serve the Jamā'at, and sacrifice financially.' All of these are caused by *Dajjāl* [Antichrist] to move you away from Allah and the Jamā'at. Therefore, the Promised Messiah[as] says that if you have taken the pledge, stay away from these snares. Do not be misled by these attractions. Remain faithful to Allah. If you turn to Him, you belong to the Promised Messiah[as] and will receive everything. The following is a beautiful admonition of the Holy Prophet[sa] in this respect.

Ḥaḍrat Ibn-e-'Abbās[ra] has related that: I was once riding with the Holy Prophet[sa]. He said, 'My dear child, I am going to teach you a few things: Keep Allah in mind, He will safeguard you; keep Allah in mind, you will find Him nearby. When in need, ask only of Allah; if you need help, ask Him alone for help. Remember, if the whole world joins together to benefit you, it can do nothing to benefit you, except if Allah wishes and decrees it for you. And if they all join to hurt you, they can do nothing to hurt you, except if Allah decrees the harm for you. The pens have been stored away and the ink has dried."

Another version is:

Keep Allah in mind, you will find Him before you. Recognise Allah in times of ease, He will recognise you in times of hardship. Remember, what escaped you was not decreed for you; and what is decreed for you will definitely come to you. Remember, the help of Allah comes as a result of steadfastness, and times of ease and times of hardship are commingled, and every hardship is followed by times of ease. (*Sunan-ut-Tirmadhī*, Abwābu Ṣifatil Qiyāmah)

Nothing that the Holy Prophet[sa] did was against the pleasure of Allah; yet, he prayed fervently, he prayed for the pleasure of Allah.

Ḥaḍrat Muḥammad Bin Ibrāhīm[ra] narrates a *ḥadīth* from Ḥaḍrat 'Āishah[ra], 'Once I was sleeping by the side of the Holy Prophet[sa]. During a time at night I did not find him there. While searching around, my hand touched his feet while he was prostrating. He was praying, "Allah, I seek the protection of Thy pleasure against Thy displeasure; and I seek the protection of Thy forgiveness against Thy punishment. I cannot count the ways of praising Thee. You are as You have described Your Holy Self."' (*Sunan-ut-Tirmadhī*, Kitābud-Da'wāt)

Another tradition says that:

> Someone from Medina heard from Ḥaḍrat 'Abdul Wahhāb Bin al-Ward[ra] that Ḥaḍrat Mu'āwiyah[ra] wrote to Ḥaḍrat 'Āishah[ra] requesting some advice. She replied, '*Assalāmo 'Alaikum*. I have heard the Holy Prophet[sa] say, "One who seeks the pleasure of Allah, even at the cost of displeasing some people, Allah is Sufficient for him against them. But he who displeases Allah for the sake of pleasing some people, Allah hands him over to those people."' (*Sunan-ut-Tirmadhī*, Kitābuz-Zuhd)

You Are the Last Jamā'at Established by Allah

The Promised Messiah[as] writes:

> It is inevitable that you should be tried with diverse types of pain and misfortune as the faithful before you were tried. Be mindful, lest you should stumble. So long as you have a firm relationship with heaven, the earth can do you no harm. Whenever harm befalls you, it will be through yourself and not through your enemy. Even if you lose all honour on earth, Allah will bestow eternal honour upon you from heaven. So do not let go of Him. It is inevitable that you be persecuted and suffer many disappointments, but do not lose heart, for it is Allah Who tests you whether you are steadfast in His cause or not. If you desire that angels should praise you in heaven, then endure beating and be joyful, hear abuse and be grateful, experience failure and do not cut your relationship with Allah. You are the last Jamā'at of Allah, so practice virtue at its

highest level. Anyone from among you who becomes slothful will be cast out of the Jamā'at like a foul thing and will die in sorrow and will be able to do no harm to Allah. I give you the good news that your God truly exists. All are His creatures, but He chooses the one who chooses Him. He comes to the one who goes to Him. He bestows honour upon him who honours Him. (*Kashti-e-Nūḥ, Rūḥānī Khazā'in*, vol. 19, p. 15)

Then the Promised Messiah[as] says:

What we need to do is to please Allah. That requires sincerity, truthfulness, and fidelity, not that the efforts of our Jamā'at be limited to mere verbiage. When Allah is pleased with us, He puts blessings in our affairs and opens the doors of His grace and blessings.... This narrow gate—the gate of truthfulness and fidelity—is not easy to cross. We can never be boastful that we start receiving dreams or revelations and thus we sit idly and refrain from utmost striving. Allah the Almighty does not like that.... (*Al-Badr*, vol., 3, No. 18–19, May 8–16, 1904)

Then he says:

Every true believer passes through such circumstances. If he becomes His with sincerity and fidelity, Allah becomes his friend. But if the structure of faith is weak, there are dangers. We have no knowledge of the secrets of anybody's heart... but anyone who totally belong to God receives His protection. Although He is the God of everyone, He manifests especially to those who hand themselves over to God. To hand oneself over to God means that the self be totally demolished and nothing should remain of it. That is why I tell my Jamā'at again and again that they should take no pride in taking the pledge. If the heart is not purified, there is no merit in placing their hands in my hand.... But anyone who makes a true pledge attains forgiveness of even major sins and receives a new life. (*Malfūẓāt*, new ed., vol. 3, p. 65)

Those Who Belong to the Promised Messiah Cannot be Separated From Him

Then the Promised Messiah[as] says:

He who does not wish to follow me can depart from me. I do not know how many terrible and thorny forests I may have to cross. Why do those who are tender-footed put themselves to trouble with me? Those who are mine will not depart from me, neither on account of misfortune, nor in consequence of the vilification of people, nor through heavenly trials and tribulations. Those who are not mine, vain are their affirmations of friendship, for they will soon be separated from me and their last state will be worse than their first. Shall we be afraid of earthquakes; shall we become frightened by trials in the cause of Allah? Can we be separated by any trial that comes from our Beloved Allah? Certainly not, but only through His grace and mercy. Those who wish to depart may do so; we bid them farewell. But they should remember that after thinking ill and cutting asunder, if they should again incline towards me, such inclination would not receive the honour from God as is bestowed upon the faithful, for the stain of ill-thinking and treachery is a big stain. (*Anwār-ul-Islām, Rūḥānī Khazā'in*, vol. 9, p. 23–24)

Steadfastness

One hundred years ago, two elders of the Jamā'at demonstrated perfect fidelity and steadfastness. They were true to their pledge, very true. They were enticed with different kinds of attractions to break the pledge, but these princes of steadfastness paid no attention to them and remained true to their pledge. The Promised Messiah[as] has paid excellent tribute to them. They are Ṣāḥibzādah Sayyed 'Abdul Laṭīf Shahīd[ra] and 'Abdur-Raḥmān Khān[ra]. I present an excerpt from the Promised Messiah[as]:

> Ponder with faith and fairness that if a Jamā'at were based entirely on deceit, falsehood, and trickery, could its members demonstrate such steadfastness and valour that they should not forsake this path, accept being trampled under stones and—not worrying about their wives and children—offer their lives despite the repeated promises of release on condition of renouncing *bai'at*? Sheikh 'Abdur-Raḥmān[ra] was slaughtered in Kabul in the same manner. He made no protest nor begged for release by renouncing *bai'at*.

This alone is the sign of a true faith and a true *Imām*. When someone attains a true understanding and the heart is permeated with spiritual sweetness, such a person does not fear being killed in this path. Of course, those whose faith are skin-deep, and faith has not permeated their limbs and veins, can turn apostate like Judas Iscariot. There are examples of such apostates in the life of every Prophet. Thanks to Allah

> that a large party of the faithful is with me; every one of them is a sign for me. This is the Grace of my Lord.
>
> رَبِّ اِنَّکَ جَنَّتِیْ وَ رَحْمَتُکَ جُنَّتِیْ وَآیَاتُکَ غِذَائِیْ
> وَفَضْلُکَ رِدَائِیْ
>
> (*Ḥaqīqat-ul-Waḥyi, Rūḥānī Khazā'in*, vol. 22, p. 360–361)

Translation:

> O my Lord, You are my Paradise, and Your Mercy is my protection, and Your signs are my nourishment and Your Grace is my mantle.

The history of the Aḥmadiyyah Muslim Jamā'at over the last one hundred years bears witness that such examples of faithfulness and fidelity have been repeatedly demonstrated. There were losses of lives and property. There were martyrdoms. Children were killed in the presence of fathers, and fathers were killed in the presence of children. Then did Allah—Who is the Greatest in rewarding faithfulness—permit this blood to be spilled in vain? No. He showered His Mercy upon their progenies in an unprecedented way. Many of you who are present here or are spread in many countries are personal witnesses to this. Indeed, many of you are the recipients of these blessings. This is a consequence of the fidelity that you have shown towards Allah and the way you remained true to the pledge of allegiance. When the time of ease comes, do not forget this pledge of *bai'at* nor let your future generations forget it. Always remain faithful to the dear Allah, so that His blessings may continue to pour on your future generations; transfer this relationship of fidelity to the coming generations.

CONDITION VI

That he/she shall refrain from following un-Islāmic customs and lustful inclinations and shall completely submit himself/herself to the authority of the Holy Qur'ān; and that he/she shall make the Word of God and the sayings of the Holy Prophet Muḥammad[sa] his/her guiding principles in every walk of his/her life.

The Promised Messiah[as] admonishes us not to follow the un-Islāmic customs that people have added to their faith because of the influence of the society in which they live. These customs have been adopted from other religions. For example, there are some frivolous customs during celebrations of marriage—like showing off the dowery given to the bride by her groom's family, or the gifts brought by them, or publicly displaying the dowery given to the bride by her own family. There is quite a show. Islām only enjoins *ḥaq mehr* [bride's due right] to be publicly announced as a part of the religious marriage ceremony. All other customs are frivolous. First, when showing off the dowery from either side, those who are well-off want to show that they are giving more than their counterparts did in their marriage. All of this is worldly competition and show.

These days, there are many among you whom Allah the Almighty has blessed greatly after migration[61]. This is one of the blessings of joining the Jamā'at of the Promised Messiah[as]. It is a consequence of the sacrifices made by your forefathers and a blessing resulting from the supplications offered by them. But there are some who, instead of being thankful by bowing before Allah the Almighty and spending in His way, become a prey to self-exultation and demonstration by excessive spending in marriages.

A lot of food is wasted in marriage celebrations and *walimahs* [reception given by husband after the marriage has been consummated]. Many dishes are prepared for public display. As a consequence, those who are not so well-off go into debt in order to have bridal dowery to display publicly. Some parents have to go into debt for fear of criticisms from their in-laws that their daughter has not brought much dowery with her. The groom's family should fear Allah. Do not permit your poor in-laws to go into debt in order to maintain your own false sense of self-esteem because the claim you make is that you are Aḥmadīs and are committed to abide by the ten conditions of *bai'at*.

---

61. The reference is to members of the Jamā'at who have migrated from the rule of oppressive Islāmic governments to western countries for religious freedom.

I have thus far briefly mentioned one custom during marriage. If I elaborate upon the subject further, I can cite many other prevailing customs during marriage ceremonies.

When the customs take root, their victim is blinded and gradually comes fully into the grip of carnal desires, whereas the pledge during *bai'at* is that he/she will safeguard completely from the carnal desires and will be completely subservient to the sovereignty of Allah and the Holy Prophet[sa]. What do Allah and His Apostle expect from us? Only that we forsake frivolous customs and abide by the commandments of Allah.

Allah the Almighty says in the Holy Qur'ān:[62]

فَاِنْ لَّمْ يَسْتَجِيْبُوْا لَكَ فَاعْلَمْ اَنَّمَا يَتَّبِعُوْنَ اَهْوَآءَهُمْ .وَمَنْ اَضَلُّ
مِمَّنِ اتَّبَعَ هَوٰهُ بِغَيْرِ هُدًى مِّنَ اللّٰهِ اِنَّ اللّٰهَ لَا يَهْدِى الْقَوْمَ الظّٰلِمِيْنَ

> But if they do not accept this invitation of yours, then know that they only follow their own evil inclinations. And who is more erring than he who follows his evil inclinations without any guidance from Allah? Verily Allah guides not the unjust people.

In this verse Allah the Almighty has given a very clear verdict that should make us fearful: those who follow their vain desires will never be rightly guided.

We claim that we have recognised and accepted the *Imām* of the Age but despite taking a pledge with the *Imām* to forsake all vain customs we are clinging to them. Everyone should examine himself: Are we taking retrograde steps? If we are true to the pledge and—fearing our Lord, eschewing carnal

62. Al-Qaṣaṣ, 28:51

desires—we turn to our Beloved Allah and praise Him, He gives us the glad tiding of Paradise.

As Almighty Allah says in the Holy Qur'ān:[63]

وَاَمَّا مَنْ خَافَ مَقَامَ رَبِّهٖ وَنَهَى النَّفْسَ عَنِ الْهَوٰى. فَاِنَّ الْجَنَّةَ هِيَ الْمَاْوٰى

But as for him who fears the station of his Lord, and restrains his soul from evil desires, the Paradise shall surely be *his* home.

I will present a few *aḥādīth* pertaining to the topic of rituals and customs.

Ḥaḍrat 'Āishah[ra] has related that the Holy Prophet[sa] said, 'An innovation in religion which has nothing to do with matters of faith is to be rejected and is unacceptable.' (*Ṣaḥīḥ Al-Bukhārī*, Kitāb-uṣ-Ṣulḥi, Bābu Izaṣṭalaḥū 'alā ṣulḥin jaurin)

Ḥaḍrat Jābir[ra] relates that the Holy Prophet[sa] addressed us and his eyes were showing redness, his voice became louder, and he was very excited as if he was warning us of an invading army. He said, 'The enemy is about to attack you any time during the day or night.' He also said, 'I and the Hour have been sent in close proximity.' (He joined his two fingers to demonstrate the closeness while he said this.) Then he added, 'Now I tell you that the best discourse is the Book of Allah and the best guidance is the guidance given by Muḥammad[sa]. The most evil thing is to introduce innovations in religion; and every innovation leads to error.' (*Ṣaḥīḥ Muslim,* Kitāb-ul-Jumu'ati, Bābu Takhfīfiṣ-Ṣalāti wal-Khuṭbati)

63. Al-Nāzi'āt, 79:41–42

Ḥaḍrat 'Amr Bin al-'Auf[ra] has narrated that the Holy Prophet[sa] said, 'The person who revives any one of my *sunnah* so that others start practicing it, he will reap the reward equal to all those persons' rewards who act upon that *sunnah*, and their reward shall remain with them as well. The person who introduces an innovation and others adopt it, he shall share in the sins of all those who act on it, and their sins will remain with them as well.' (*Sunano Ibn-e-Mājah*, Bābu man Aḥyā Sunnata qad umītat)

Evolving Innovations and Rituals Deserve to be Rejected

In short, the Holy Prophet[sa] told us in the above-quoted *aḥadīth* that those innovations that have nothing to do with faith, which take one away from faith, which disrespect the commandments of Allah and His Apostle, are all worthy of rejection. They are all useless and ought to be shunned. Stay away from them because they will gradually corrupt faith.

You can see that innovations have taken a firm foothold in other religions and have corrupted them. This, indeed, was bound to happen because it was destined that Islām should remain the only living faith. But if you make a close examination you will find that other religions such as Christianity—despite being one religion—have made many local customs in different countries as a part of faith in that country. We observe the same phenomenon in Africa. When the path of innovations is opened, new innovations continue to creep up.

The Holy Prophet[sa] has expressed grave concern and has given severe warnings to those who create innovations in matters of religion. He was very concerned about it. A *ḥadīth* relates that he said, 'I am terrified at the thought of you falling prey to these innovations and lustful inclinations. I am afraid that this may cause great harm to the religion and may lead you astray!'

These days, you are living in Western societies that have many customs and rituals of their own which can create distance between you and your religion and that can diminish the beauty of Islāmic teachings for you. The lustre of worldliness is far more attractive; therefore, there is need for great caution at every step. Instead of adopting their wrong customs, we must present the beautiful teachings of Islām. Each Aḥmadī should possess such a strong character that Western culture should have no effect on him/her whatsoever. For instance, women are enjoined to observe *purdah* [the veil] according to Islāmic teachings. It is in the interest of a woman's integrity that she attains a prominent status in society due to the fact that she observes Islāmic *purdah*. When a woman observes *purdah* willingly and she herself tells others the benefits of this Islāmic injunction, it will have a far greater impact on others as compared to men who propagate the advantage of *purdah* in this society. Those women who observe *purdah* acquire many more chances to perform *tablīgh* due to their unique prominence in society. This matter requires great attention.

There exist many other social evils in Western society. To adopt them merely because we live in this society and we feel compelled to do so is, indeed, a worrisome situation. For instance, it is wrong on your part to befriend someone who consumes alcohol and to accompany him to a restaurant or a bar thinking that: 'he would drink alcohol but I will drink coffee or some other beverage.' Great caution is required. One day, you may be influenced by him to try just one sip and then God forbid, it becomes your habit to drink. Keep the following *ḥadīth* of the Holy Prophet[sa] in mind:

> Ḥaḍrat Abū Barzah[ra] relates that the Holy Prophet[sa] said, 'I fear that you may be tempted by the lusts of the flesh and sexual cravings, and I am afraid of the evil consequences of sensual temptations.' (*Musnadu Aḥmadabni Ḥanbal*, vol. 4. p. 423, printed in Beirut)

The Promised Messiah[as] says:

> Until a man truly endeavours and works hard, he cannot attain the treasure of divine understanding which Islām contains and which brings a death upon the life tainted by sin. Allah the Almighty says very clearly:[64]
>
> وَاَمَّامَنْ خَافَ مَقَامَ رَبِّهٖ وَنَهَى النَّفْسَ عَنِ الْهَوٰى. فَاِنَّ الْجَنَّةَ هِيَ الْمَاْوٰى
>
> It is easy for someone to boast that he believes in God, and despite this claim, to lack altogether the impact caused by real belief. Such a claim would be utter nonsense. Such people have no regard for God, and God cares for them not. (*Al-Ḥakam*, vol. 9, No. 29, August 17, 1905, p. 6)

64. But as for him who fears to stand before his Lord, and restrains his soul from evil desires, the Garden shall surely be *his* home. Al-Nāzi'āt, 79:41–42

Then he says:

> One who is fearful of standing before God and secures himself against the selfish desires attains the station of Paradise. To secure oneself against the carnal desires is the death of the ego. By doing so, one can please God in this very world and thereby attain Paradise. (*Al-Badr*, vol. 1, August 3, 1905, p. 2)

The Holy Qur'ān is Our Guide to Islāmic Teachings

Refraining from unwanted customs and rituals, and restraining oneself from lustful inclinations, are indeed part of Islāmic teachings. To comprehend this teaching, we turn towards the Holy Qur'ān as our Guide. The truth of the matter is that if a believer adopts the Holy Qur'ān as the source of guidance in his daily life, all his evils will start vanishing automatically. His heart shall contain no lustful desires because this is the pure Book which completes the *sharī'ah* as a way of life. Keeping in view all facets of human life, Allah the Almighty revealed this Book to the pure heart of the Holy Prophet[sa]. And then whenever it was required, the Holy Prophet[sa] expounded upon the teachings through his practices, actions, and sayings. That is the reason why the Promised Messiah[as] has instructed us to accept the Book as fully binding upon us. I would, therefore, like to present references from the Qur'ān, the *ḥadīth* and some writings of the Promised Messiah[as] with respect to this topic.

Allah the Almighty says:[65]

وَلَقَدْ يَسَّرْنَا الْقُرْآنَ لِلذِّكْرِ فَهَلْ مِنْ مُّدَّكِرٍ

And indeed We have made the Holy Qur'ān easy *to understand and* to remember. But is there anyone who would receive admonition?

There is a *ḥadīth*:

Ḥaḍrat Abū Mūsā al-Ash'arī[ra] relates that the Holy Prophet[sa] said, 'The example of a believer who recites the Qur'ān and acts accordingly is like that of a citron that tastes good and smells good. And a believer who does not recite the Qur'ān but acts upon it is like a date, which is good in taste but has no smell. And the example of a hypocrite who recites the Qur'ān is like the basil, which smells good, but tastes bitter. And the example of a hypocrite who neither recites the Qur'ān nor acts upon it is like the colocynth, which tastes bitter and has bad smell.' (*Ṣaḥīḥ Al-Bukhārī*, Kitābu Faḍā'ilil-Qur'ān, Bābu Ithmi man ra'ā bi-Qirā'atil-Qur'ānī au ta'akkala bihi au fakhura bih)

The Promised Messiah[as] says:

...the Holy Qur'ān is filled with deep points of wisdom. It excels the Bible in every way in teaching true goodness. In particular, the lamp that shows the Real and Unchangeable Allah is held by none other than the Qur'ān. Allah knows how many would have fallen victim to the worship of creatures if Qur'ān had not been revealed. Thanks to Allah that

65. Al-Qamar, 54:18

the Unity that had disappeared from the world has been re-established. (*Toḥfah-e-Qaiṣariyyah, Rūḥānī Khazā'in*, vol. 12, p. 282)

Your Life Lies in the Holy Qur'ān

Then the Promised Messiah[as] says:

> Do not leave the Holy Qur'ān as a forsaken thing because therein lies your life. Those who honour the Holy Qur'ān will be the honoured ones in Heaven. Those who gives precedence to the Qur'ān over every *ḥadīth* and saying will be granted precedence in heaven. There is no book for humanity on the face of the earth except the Qur'ān; and there is no Messenger and Intercessor for the children of Adam except Muḥammad, the Chosen one, may peace and blessings of Allah be upon him. (*Kashti-e-Nūḥ, Rūḥānī Khazā'in*, vol. 19, p. 13)

The Promised Messiah[as] also says:

> The Holy Qur'ān attracts its true followers with its spiritual qualities and inherent light. It illumines their hearts and then manifests mighty signs to establish such a strong bond with God as cannot be broken by a cutting sword. It opens the eye of the heart and closes the dirty pond of sin. It grants the blessing of delicious converse with Allah and grants knowledge of the Unseen. It informs the supplicant of the acceptance of prayers. Anyone who opposes a true follower of the Holy Qur'ān, is shown by the mighty signs of Almighty Allah

that Allah is with His servant who follows His Book. (*Chashmah-e-Ma'rifat, Rūḥānī Khazā'in*, vol. 23, p. 308–309)

Then he says:

Beware! Do not take a single step in contravention of Allah's teaching and the Guidance contained in the Qur'ān. Verily, I tell you truly that whosoever evades even the least of the seven hundred commandments embodied in the Holy Qur'ān, he slams the door of salvation upon himself. Only the Holy Qur'ān has opened the real and perfect paths of salvation; all others were only its shadows. Therefore, you should study this Holy Scripture with the utmost attention and deepest thought; and you should love it as you have never loved anything else. For indeed, as God has conveyed to me:

اَلْخَيْرُ كُلُّهُ فِى الْقُرْآن

All kinds of goodness in contained in the Qur'ān—and this is the truth. Unfortunate, indeed, are those who give preference to other things over it. The Holy Qur'ān is the fountainhead for all your success and salvation. There is not even a single religious need that has not been provided for you in this Holy Book. On the Day of Judgement, the Holy Qur'ān will attest to or falsify your faith; and apart from the Qur'ān there is no other book under heavens that can provide you with guidance without a reference to the Qur'ān. It is, indeed, a great blessing of God that He has bestowed a book like this upon you. Verily, I tell you truly that the book that has been read to you, had it been read to the Christians, they would not have perished; and the blessing and guidance that have been vouch-safed upon you, had they been extended to the Jews in place of the Torah, some of their sects would not have ended up denying the Day of Judgement. Realise, therefore, the value of the blessing bestowed upon you. It is a precious blessing, and a great treasure. Without the Holy Qur'ān, the whole world would have been no better than a dirty clot of half-formed flesh. Indeed, it is a book compared to which all other sources of guidance amount to nothing at all. (*Kashti-e-Nūḥ, Rūḥānī Khazā'in*, vol. 19, p. 26–27)

Everyone of us should analyse as to what extent he loves the Holy Qur'ān and obeys its commandments and tries to practice them in his life. There are ways of manifesting love. The most important thing for an Aḥmadī is to make it obligatory upon him to recite a minimum of two or three *rukū'*[66] of the Holy Qur'ān regularly. Then, taking the next step, he should read it with translation. By reciting the Holy Qur'ān daily along with reading the translation, its beautiful teachings subconsciously infiltrate into the deep layers of the mind.

Another matter enjoined by the Promised Messiah[as] in the sixth condition is to adopt the ordinances of Allah and His Apostle as a code of life in every matter and to refer to them whenever the need arises. This is not mere lip-service. If you ponder over this directive, it will cause great concern. Allah the Almighty says:[67]

66. The Holy Qur'ān is divided, for the convenience of recitation into 30 *parahs* (parts), and each *pārah* is divided into *rukū'*.
67. Al-Nisā', 4:60

يٰٓاَيُّهَا الَّذِيْنَ اٰمَنُوْٓا اَطِيْعُوا اللّٰهَ وَاَطِيْعُوا الرَّسُوْلَ وَ اُولِى الْاَمْرِ مِنْكُمْ
فَاِنْ تَنَازَعْتُمْ فِى شَىْءٍ فَرُدُّوْهُ اِلَى اللّٰهِ وَالرَّسُوْلِ اِنْ كُنْتُمْ تُؤْمِنُوْنَ
بِاللّٰهِ وَالْيَوْمِ الْاٰخِرِ ذٰلِكَ خَيْرٌ وَّاَحْسَنُ تَاْوِيْلًا

O ye who believe! obey Allah, and obey *His* Messenger and those who are in authority over you. And if you differ in anything among yourselves, refer it to Allah and *His* Messenger if you are believers in Allah and the Last Day. That is best and most commendable in the end.

Again, He says:[68]

اَطِيْعُوا اللّٰهَ وَالرَّسُوْلَ لَعَلَّكُمْ تُرْحَمُوْنَ

And obey Allah and the Messenger that you may be shown mercy.

Again, He says:[69]

يَسْـَٔلُوْنَكَ عَنِ الْاَنْفَالِ. قُلِ الْاَنْفَالُ لِلّٰهِ وَالرَّسُوْلِ. فَاتَّقُوا اللّٰهَ
وَاَصْلِحُوْا ذَاتَ بَيْنِكُمْ وَاَطِيْعُوا اللّٰهَ وَرَسُوْلَهٗ اِنْ كُنْتُمْ مُّؤْمِنِيْنَ

They ask thee concerning the spoils *of wars*. Say, 'The spoils belong to Allah and the Messenger. So fear Allah, and set things right among yourselves, and obey Allah and His Messenger, if you are believers.

In these verses, Allah the Almighty directs us to earnestly obey His commandments and to practise them sincerely. We are also instructed to act according to the explanation of these

68. Āl-e-'Imrān, 3:133
69. Al-Anfāl, 8:2

commandments provided by the Holy Prophet[sa]. Exhibit full obedience to the appointed leaders and the organisation of the Community; only then it can be said that you have truthfully fulfilled your dues to your *bai'at*.

I will now present some *aḥādīth* on this subject.

Ḥaḍrat 'Ubādah Bin Aṣ-Ṣāmit[ra] narrates, 'We made a solemn pledge at the hand of the Messenger of Allah on the condition that we will pay heed to and obey all his directives whether we like them or not.' (*Ṣaḥīḥ Al-Bukhārī*, Kitābul-Aḥkām, Bābu Kaifa Yubāyi'ul-Imāmun-Nāsa)

'Abdur-Raḥmān Bin 'Amr As-Salamī and Ḥaḍrat Ḥujr Bin Ḥujr said, 'We went to 'Irbāḍ Bin Sāriyah[ra] who said, "One day the Apostle of Allah led us in the morning Prayer, then gave us a very effective and eloquent exhortation at which the eyes shed tears and the hearts became fearful. A man among the audience said, 'O Apostle of Allah! It seems as if it were a farewell exhortation! So, what injunction do you give us?' He then said, 'I enjoin you to fear Allah, hear and obey even if your *Amīr* [Leader] be an Abyssinian slave, for a time is coming that those of you who live after me will see great disagreement. You must then follow my rightly guided *khulafā'* [caliphs] and me. Stick to it and hold fast to it. You have to avoid innovations in the religion, for every innovations introduced in the name of religion is an undesirable one, and every innovation is a manifest error.'" (*Sunan-ut-Tirmadhī*, Kitābul 'Ilmi Bābul Akhdhi Bis Sunnah. Also *Sunano Abī Dāwūd*, Kitāb-us-Sunnati, Bābu Luzūmis Sunnah)

We, the Aḥmadīs who claim complete obedience to the Holy Prophet[sa] and declare our absolute faith, should always keep this advice and the *ḥadīth* in our minds.

> Ḥaḍrat Anas[ra] narrates that the Holy Prophet[sa] said, 'Whoever possesses the following three qualities will taste the sweet delight of faith: first, Allah and His Apostle become dearer to him than anything else. Second, he loves a person only for the sake of Allah's love! Third, he hates to revert to disbelief as he hates to be thrown into the fire!' (*Ṣaḥīḥ Al-Bukhārī*, Kitābul-Īmān, Bābu Halāwatil Īmān)

The Promised Messiah[as] says:

> Look, Allah the Almighty says in the Holy Qur'ān:[70]
>
> قُلْ اِنْ كُنْتُمْ تُحِبُّوْنَ اللّٰهَ فَاتَّبِعُوْنِىْ يُحْبِبْكُمُ اللّٰهُ
>
> The only way to please Allah the Almighty is to be fully obedient to the Holy Prophet[sa]; and there is no other way that will lead you to the communion with God. The final objective of man should always be to find the One God who is without any partner. He should shun associating anyone with God and indulging in innovations! He should be obeying the Messenger[sa] and not following his personal lusts and base desires. Listen, I say it again: Man cannot succeed in any other way but by treading the true path of the Messenger[sa] of Allah.
>
> We have only one Messenger[sa]; and only one Holy Qur'ān was revealed to that Messenger[sa]—obeying whom we can find

70. Say, 'If you love Allah, follow me: *then* will Allah love you... Āl-e-'Imrān, 3:32

God. The innovations introduced by the present day *fuqarā'* [hermits] and the methods of *durūd* and *waẓā'if* [prayer incantations] invented by the leaders of the hermitages are all a tool that leads a man astray. Stay away from them. These people have tried to break the Seal of the Prophets and in a way have made a different *sharī'ah*. You should remember that the key for opening the door of Allah's blessings and grace is only to adhere to the injunctions of the Holy Qur'ān and to follow the Holy Prophet[sa] and to establish Prayer and keep fasting in the established manner. That person is lost who adopts any new path instead of following those established ways. That person shall end up dying in failure who does not comply with the dictates of Allah and His Messenger and walks divergent paths. (*Malfūẓāt*, new ed., vol. 3, p. 102–103)

The Promised Messiah[as] again says:

Almighty Allah says in the Holy Qur'ān:[71]

قُلْ اِنْ كُنْتُمْ تُحِبُّوْنَ اللّٰهَ فَاتَّبِعُوْنِىْ يُحْبِبْكُمُ اللّٰهُ

The only way to please Allah the Almighty is to be fully obedient to the Holy Prophet[sa]. It is a common observation that people have become a slave to and are entangled in various kinds of customs. When someone dies, instead of praying for the deceased, as they should, they perform various rituals that are innovations. These customs are contrary to the teachings of the Holy Prophet[sa]. Carrying them out is disrespectful to him in the sense that his

71. Say, 'If you love Allah, follow me: *then* will Allah love you… Āl-e-'Imrān, 3:32

teachings are not considered to be sufficient and final. Otherwise, there was no need to introduce these customs. (*Malfūẓāt*, new ed., vol. 3, p. 316)

Then he says:

> This temporary life will come to an end—whether spent in constrained circumstances or times of ease. But the matter of the Hereafter is very hard. It is an everlasting abode that has no end in time. If one goes to that life in a condition that one's affairs with Allah are straight, and the fear of Allah had overpowered one's heart, and with repentance from sins, he had secured himself from everything that Allah has designated as sin, the Grace of Allah will guide him. He will be pleased with his Lord, and his Lord will be pleased with him. But if one does not do so and spends this life in heedlessness, his end is dangerous. Therefore, at the time of *bai'at*, make a firm determination of what *bai'at* is and what benefits it provides. If it is done merely for worldly objectives, it is useless. But if it is for the sake of faith and pleasure of Allah, then it is blessed and carries its real aims and objectives. It can be hoped that it will provide all the benefits that the true *bai'at* provides. (*Malfūẓāt*, new ed., vol. 6, p. 142)

May Allah enable us to accept the Promised Messiah[as] as the *Imām* of this Age from the core of our heart! With great pain and care he wanted to prepare a Jamā'at for establishing the Kingdom of God and His Messenger, and advised us with anguish in his heart. May Allah make us deserving of what he wanted us to be, and may we fully comply with all the conditions of the pledge of *bai'at*. May we act upon them, and always keep them before our eyes. No action of ours should make us guilty of contradicting the teachings of the Promised Messiah[as], and we should always be examining our deeds.

May Allah the Almighty help us.

Today, with the grace of Allah the Almighty, after *du'ā'*. this Convention[72] will reach its end. May we for the entire year, rather for the entire life, be the recipients of the blessings and spiritual benefits of this Convention. May Allah cultivate and maintain the bond of love in our coming generations for Allah, His Messenger, the Promised Messiah[as] and *khilāfat.* May Allah expose not our past shortcomings and sins, and may He forgive us, and may He, out of His sheer Grace, keep us among the Jamā'at of His dear ones. Our Allah! You are Forgiving and Merciful. Forgive our sins. Take mercy on us. Take us under the cover of Your forgiveness and mercy. Never allow us to depart from You. *Āmīn, yā Rabbal 'Alamīn*[73]*!*

72. Reference is to the concluding address delivered at the Annual Convention of the Aḥmadiyyah Muslim Jamā'at, Germany, on August 24, 2003.
73. Accept our supplication, O Lord of All the Worlds.

CONDITION VII

That he/she shall entirely give up pride and vanity and shall pass all his/her life in humbleness, cheerfulness, forbearance and meekness.

[From the Friday sermon delivered at Frankfurt, Germany, on August 29, 2003, in which seventh and eighth conditions of bai'at were discussed in detail.]

Next to Shirk, There is no Calamity Like Arrogance

After exhibiting his pride, Satan had decided from the very beginning that he would try his utmost to hinder men from becoming true servants of Allah. He had made up his mind to entrap mankind through various ways. Even when man would perform a virtuous act, Satan would make him self-conceited, and thus through his personal vanity and egotism, he could be led to be proud and arrogant. This sense of pride would, in the end, make man lose the reward of his virtuous act. Satan himself disobeyed Allah's command due to his personal vanity. Therefore, from day one, through the use of this very tool in its various forms, he resolved to lead man astray from the right path. Only the servants of the Gracious God, who are His special servants and are engaged in His worship, generally remain unharmed of Satan's attack. Otherwise, it is through the trap of pride that Satan usually succeeds in holding mankind in his captivity.

One must not take it lightly that we accepted the condition at the time of making *bai'at* that we would not indulge in pride and vanity. Give up arrogance in its entirety. It is not easy. Arrogance has many diverse forms. Satan attacks mankind utilizing different methods. It is an extremely terrifying state! Actually, it is only through the Grace of Allah that one can be saved from it. Therefore, in the seventh condition, the Promised Messiah[as] also introduced a way to obtain Allah's Graces. He said if we try to break away from the habit of arrogance, but do not fill in the emptiness with humility and meekness, then arrogance would attack us again. Therefore, adopt humbleness! Allah the Almighty loves the way of humility. The Promised Messiah[as] himself demonstrated humbleness to such an extent that it has no parallel. That is the reason that Allah the Almighty was so pleased with him that He said to him in a revelation: (Urdu) 'He liked your humble ways!' We claim to have made *bai'at* with the Promised Messiah[as], and we have accepted him as the *Imām* of the Age. Therefore, it is all the more important for us to adopt this moral quality.

Man has no reason to show arrogance and haughtiness. In the Holy Qur'ān Allah the Almighty says:[74]

وَلَا تَمْشِ فِی الْاَرْضِ مَرَحًا. اِنَّکَ لَنْ تَخْرِقَ الْاَرْضَ وَلَنْ تَبْلُغَ الْجِبَالَ طُوْلًا

And walk not in the earth haughtily, for thou canst not rend the earth, nor canst thou reach the mountains in height.

This verse makes it clear that man has no position at all to strut about. What is it that he is so proud of? Some people think they are the kings of the time. They do not wish to come out of their limited circle. Remaining within their limited circles, they think of themselves as something grand. I am going to give the example of the smallest circle—that of domestic circumstances. It is truly alarming to see how savagely some men mistreat their wives and children. Some girls write to me telling me they have now become adults, but since their childhood they have been witnessing the oppressive treatment of their fathers towards their mothers and themselves, but now they cannot tolerate it any more. They used to hide in their rooms as soon as their father entered the house. If their mother or anyone of them happened to say anything against his likings, the father was so cruel that he would beat them. It is only arrogance that has turned fathers like this to commit such extremities. Most of them keep a nice posture outside their homes and people think no one is as noble as those persons. Thus, the outsiders have a favourable opinion about them. But there are some who keep an

74. Banī Isrā'īl, 17:38

arrogant attitude both inside and outside of their homes, and their condition is obviously well known to all. Consequently, on coming of age, the children of such ill-mannered and arrogant men, especially their sons, show a reaction to their father's cruelty to their mothers, sisters or themselves. They start confronting their father, and when the time comes when the father becomes weak in his old age, they take their revenge. There are several circles in society, and the circle of domestic affairs is only one of them. There is also a social circle outside the home. If you take a survey, you will continuously discover such examples of arrogance in all these circles.

The extreme form of arrogance is found in the wider circle: due to arrogance some nations, countries, and governments look down upon the rest. They despise poor nations and countries. Today, this is a major cause of disorder and trouble in the world. If the arrogance is eliminated, disorder shall disappear, but the arrogant nations and governments do not realise that when Allah the Almighty decides to break the disdainful attitude of the haughty, they disappear forever from the face of the earth.

Allah the Almighty says in the Holy Qur'ān:[75]

فَلَا تُصَعِّرْ خَدَّكَ لِلنَّاسِ وَلَا تَمْشِ فِي الْأَرْضِ مَرَحًا. إِنَّ اللّٰهَ لَا يُحِبُّ كُلَّ مُخْتَالٍ فَخُوْرٍ

> And do not puff up your cheek before men in pride nor walk in the earth haughtily; surely, Allah loves not any arrogant boaster.

75. Luqmān, 31:19

As is evident from this verse, Allah the Almighty says that we should not walk around displaying pride and arrogance. The proud people have a special style of their own. Allah does not like a stiff-necked person walking around. Some people habitually stand proudly in front of their subordinates, but they show humbleness in front of their superiors. The evil of hypocrisy is evident in such persons. Thus, the trait of arrogance breeds many other evils; slowly and gradually all paths of virtue are fully closed. Such persons drift away from religion and also from the *Niẓām-e-Jamā'at* [Organisation of the Jamā'at]. As their arrogance increases, they move further away from the nearness and blessings of Allah and His Messenger.

It is mentioned in one *ḥadīth*:

> Ḥaḍrat Jābir[ra] narrated that the Holy Prophet[sa] said, 'On the Day of Judgement the dearest to me, the closest to me, shall be those who are the best in good morals. And those among you shall be most severely under the wrath and farthest from me who are *tharthār*, those who are foul-mouthed and vain babblers; *mutashaddiq*, those who talk making wry faces and distend their cheeks; and *mutfaihiq*.' The Companions[ra] asked, 'O Messenger[sa] of Allah! We know the meaning of *tharthār*, and *matashaddiq*, but who are the *mutfaihiq*? He replied, '*Mutfaihiq* are those who speak haughtily, arrogantly.' (*Sunan-ut-Tirmadhī*, Abwāb-ul-Birri waṣ-Ṣilah, Bābu fī Ma'ālil Akhlāq)

> Ḥaḍrat Ibn-e-Mas'ūd[ra] narrated that the Holy Prophet[sa] said, 'Three things are the roots of every sin. One should avoid them. Refrain from arrogance because it was due to arrogance that Satan was instigated not to prostrate to Adam. Second,

stay away from greed because it was greed that made Adam eat the fruit of the forbidden tree. Third, avoid jealousy because it was out of jealously that one of Adam's sons killed his brother.' (*Ar-Risālah Al-Qushairiyyah*, Bāb-ul-Ḥasadi, p. 79)

Ḥaḍrat 'Abdullāh Bin Mas'ūd[ra] narrated that the Holy Prophet[sa] said, 'One whose heart has arrogance as little as a small grain will not be allowed to enter Paradise.' One man said, 'O Prophet of Allah! Man wishes to be well-dressed, to have good shoes on, and to look good.' The Holy Prophet[sa] replied, 'This is not arrogance,' adding, 'Allah the Almighty is Elegant and likes elegance, that is, He likes beauty. Real arrogance is when man rejects what is true, considers people lowly, holds them in contempt and treats them badly.' (*Ṣaḥīḥ Muslim,* Kitāb-ul-Īmān, Bābu Taḥrīmil-kibri wa Bayānīh)

Another tradition relates that:

Ḥaḍrat Abū Hurairah[ra] narrated that the Holy Prophet[sa] said, 'Heaven and Hell had a discussion and argument. Hell said that great oppressors and haughty people entered in it; Heaven said that weak and meek people entered in it. On this Allah the Almighty said to Hell, "You are the manifestation of my punishment. Through you I punish whomsoever I wish." And He said to Heaven, "You are the manifestation of my mercy. I grant mercy on whomsoever I please through you; and both of you shall have your full share that may belong to you."' (*Ṣaḥīḥ Muslim,* Kitāb-ul-Jannati wa Ṣifati Ni'amihā wa Ahlihā)

May Allah make it so that each Aḥmadī seeks mercy from Allah the Almighty by treading on the path of humility, meekness and civility, and becomes worthy of Allah's Paradise, and may each home be free from the sin of arrogance.

A *ḥadīth* recounts that:

> Ḥaḍrat Abū Sa'īd Khudrī[ra] and Ḥaḍrat Abū Hurairah[ra] related that the Holy Prophet[sa] said, 'Honour is the garment of Allah the Almighty and grandeur is His mantle.' Allah the Almighty says, "Therefore, I shall punish him who attempts to snatch them from Me."' (*Ṣaḥīḥ Muslim,* Kitāb-ul-Birri waṣ-Ṣilah)

Arrogant Shall Never Enter Paradise

So, in the long run, arrogance incites man to confront Allah. When Allah the Almighty has decreed that He shall not forgive one who associates partners with Him, then how can one who claims to be god-like be pardoned? It was indeed arrogance that created people in the mold of the Pharaoh. You have read about the end that these Pharaoh-like people met and have also witnessed some in this age. It is indeed a cause for fear; each Aḥmadī should try and avoid the slightest of arrogance because it tends to spread and completely engulf man. Allah the Almighty has given us this warning, 'This is My mantle; I am Lord of all the worlds, Grandeur belongs to Me; accept it and show humility. If you try to cross these lines, you shall be punished. Even if you have arrogance only equal to a grain, punishment is in your fate.' In conjunction with this warning, however, a glad tiding is also given. Allah says, 'I shall save you from the torment of Fire if you have the slightest degree of faith,' as is mentioned in a *ḥadīth*:

Ḥaḍrat 'Abdullāh[ra] narrates that the Holy Prophet[sa] said, 'One whose heart has arrogance only equal to a grain will not enter Paradise and one whose heart has faith only equal to a grain will not enter Fire.' (*Sunano Ibn-e-Mājah*, Kitāb-ul-Muqaddimah)

The Promised Messiah[as] says:

> I tell you truly that on the Day of Judgement after '*shirk*'—associating partners with Allah—there will be no evil like arrogance. It is an evil that disgraces man in both the worlds. Divine mercy redresses everyone who believes in the Unity of God, but not the arrogant. Satan, too, claimed to believe in One God; however, he was arrogant and contemptuous towards Adam whom God loved. Satan criticised him and was ruined, and the yoke of curse hung around his neck. So, the first sin for which a person was eternally ruined was indeed arrogance. (*Ā'īnah-e-Kamālāt-e-Islām*, *Rūḥānī Khazā'in*, vol. 5, p. 598)

He goes on to say:

> If you have any element of arrogance, hypocrisy, conceit, or indolence, then you are not worthy of acceptance. Do not deceive yourselves over a few things, in that you have achieved what you could, because God wishes that your entire being should go through a complete revolution. He demands a death from you, after which He shall give you life. (*Kashti-e-Nūḥ*, *Rūḥānī Khazā'in*, vol. 19, p. 12)

Deep Connection Between Arrogance and Satan

The Promised Messiah[as] then says:

> Indeed, there are people who, although hundreds of thousands of ranks below those of Prophets of God (peace be on them all) grow arrogant when they have offered the *ṣalāt* for a couple of days. Similarly, rather than be purified by fasting and performing *Ḥajj*, they develop conceit and arrogance. Remember, arrogance comes from Satan and makes one satanic. Until man keeps away from it, it becomes an impediment in the acceptance of truth and beneficence of the Divine. Arrogance should not be adopted in any way at all, not with regard to knowledge, not with regard to wealth, not with regard to high rank, not due to caste, ancestry and lineage. For it is mostly due to these things that arrogance develops. Unless one purifies oneself from these conceits one cannot be esteemed in the sight of Allah the Almighty. One cannot be granted the cognizance of God that burns the worthless emotional elements, for this [conceit] belongs to Satan, and Allah the Almighty does not like it…

The Promised Messiah[as] is stating that there are a few basic activities that should be avoided. Some people consider themselves most virtuous after saying the *Ṣalāt* for a few days; they adopt a strange serious facial expression exuding pride. You must have come across certain long-robed individuals with *tasbīh* [rosary] in hand coming out of mosques. Their demeanour exhibits pride and haughtiness. Thank God, the Aḥmadiyyah Muslim Jamā'at is free from such long-robed individuals. On their return from *Ḥajj*, there is tremendous propaganda. Such people fast for appearances. Their visits to perform *Ḥajj* are also for show. It is all done to feign superiority so that people may say that such a person is virtuous, fasts a lot, is a *ḥajjī*, and is most pious. All these ostentations stem out of arrogance, or arrogance develops from these ostentations.

The Promised Messiah[as] also says that some people are arrogant because of their caste or lineage: 'so and so is lower status; how could he be equal to them?' The Promised Messiah[as] stated that arrogance is of many kinds that take you away from the cognizance of Allah the Almighty, away from His nearness, and thereby in the trap of Satan.

Again, the Promised Messiah[as] says:

> Thus, in my opinion, this is a fine way to be purified. It is impossible to find a better way than to discard arrogance and pride of any sort—about learning, family or wealth. When a person is granted insight by God, he can see that every light descends from heavens and helps remove all forms of darkness. Man is always in need of heavenly light. Even the eye cannot see without the heavenly light of the sun. Similarly, the internal light that removes every kind of darkness and in its place generates the light of *taqwā* and purity also comes down from the heavens. I tell you truly that a man's righteousness, faith, and purity all descend from the heavens. It all depends on the special grace of Allah. If He wills He bestows it; and if He wills He takes it away.
>
> Thus, real cognizance is indeed that man should consider his 'self' deeply humble and most insignificant and should

seek Allah's grace with humility and meekness by falling prostrate at the Divine threshold. He begs for that light of cognizance, which destroys passions of the 'self' and develops a light within and bestows a power and enthusiasm for virtues. Then, if with Allah's Grace he finds this share and at some time acquires a clearer insight or strong conviction, he must not feel pride and conceit. Rather, he should further develop in his humility and submission, for the more insignificant he deems himself, the greater will be the experiences and Divine light from Allah the Almighty that will provide him with [spiritual] light and power.

If a man holds fast to this belief, then it is hoped that with the grace of Allah the Almighty, his moral condition shall be good. To think high of oneself in the world is also arrogance and brings about the same consequences. It grows to a point that man curses others and holds them in contempt.' (*Malfūẓāt*, new ed., vol. 4, p. 212–213)

He then states:

Arrogance is a most dangerous disease. Whoever develops this meets spiritual death. I know most certainly that this disease is worse than murder. An arrogant person turns into Satan's brother because it was arrogance alone that disgraced Satan. Therefore, it is a prerequisite for a believer that he should not have arrogance; rather, he is required to have humility and meekness. Those who are divinely appointed have humility of the highest order. The Holy Prophet[sa] had this quality more than anyone else. One of his servants was asked as to how he was treated. He replied that the truth was that he was served by the Holy Prophet[sa] more than he served him.[76]

(اللّٰهُمَّ صلّ علیٰ محمدٍ وَعلیٰ اٰل محمّدٍ وَ بارک وسلّم)

(*Malfūẓāt*, new ed., vol. 4, p. 437–438)

Arrogance is Most Displeasing in the Sight of Allah

Again, the Promised Messiah[as] says:

> …I admonish my Jamā'at to shun arrogance because arrogance is most loathsome to Allah, the Lord of Glory. You may not perhaps fully realise what arrogance is. So learn it from me because I speak with the spirit of Allah.
>
> Everyone who looks down upon his brother because he considers himself to be more learned, wise, or more accomplished is arrogant. He is arrogant because, instead of considering God to be the Fountainhead of all wisdom and knowledge, he considers himself to be something. Does God not have the power to derange him mentally and instead grant superior knowledge, wisdom, and dexterity to his brother whom he considers inferior? Likewise he too is arrogant who thinks of his wealth or high status and looks down upon his brother. He is arrogant because he has ignored the fact that it is God who has bestowed this status and grandeur on him. He is blind and does not realise that God has power

76. Bless O Allah Muḥammad and his people and grant them Thy bounties and peace.

to afflict him with such misfortune as would all of a sudden cast him to the lowest of the low; and again, He has the power to bestow greater wealth and prosperity upon that brother of his whom he considers small. Yet again, that person is arrogant who is proud of his superior bodily health, or of his handsomeness, or good looks, or strength, or prowess, and scornfully makes fun of his brother and teases him and addresses him with derisive names, not satisfied with this he advertises his physical defects. It is so because he is unaware of the existence of a God Who possesses power to suddenly afflict him with such bodily defects as may leave him much worse than his brother.

Similarly, the person who relies on his own strength, and neglects to supplicate to God, is arrogant. This is because he has not recognised Divine strengths and powers and instead considers himself to be something. Therefore, O dear ones, remember all this lest you are deemed arrogant in the sight of Allah in some manner and you are unaware of it. A person who corrects a wrong word of his brother with arrogance has also partaken in arrogance. A person who does not wish to listen to what his brother has to say with civility and turns his face away has also partaken of arrogance. He who feels disgust for a poor and needy brother who sits next to him has also partaken of arrogance. A person who looks with derision and ridicule at one who prays has also partaken from arrogance. One who does not wish to be completely obedient to God's appointee and Prophet also partakes of arrogance. One who does not listen attentively to God's appointee and Prophet and does not read his writings with care also partakes of arrogance. Therefore, try to rid yourselves of any portion

> of arrogance in you lest you be destroyed and so that you, along with your family, get salvation. Turn to God, love Him as much as it is possible to love someone in this life and fear your God as much as one may fear someone in this world. Be of pure heart and pure intention and meek, submissive and harmless so that you may be shown mercy. (*Nazūl-ul-Masīḥ*, *Rūḥānī Khazā'in*, vol. 18, p. 402–403)

The other part that has been stated in this condition is that one shall spend his life in lowliness, humbleness, cheerfulness, forbearance and meekness. As I mentioned earlier, if you try to free your heart and mind of arrogance, manage to free it, then most necessarily you would have to inculcate a higher quality, a higher characteristic, a higher attribute in you or else Satan would repeat his onslaught, for it is his task not to leave you alone. That quality is of humility and meekness. It is not possible for arrogance and meekness to co-exist. Arrogant people are always deriding and mocking humble people who are servants of the Gracious God. When confronted with such people you are not to adopt their attitude; rather, you are to abide by this commandment of Allah the Almighty:[77]

وَعِبَادُ الرَّحْمٰنِ الَّذِيْنَ يَمْشُوْنَ عَلَى الْاَرْضِ هَوْنًا وَّاِذَا خَاطَبَهُمُ الْجَاهِلُوْنَ قَالُوْا سَلٰمًا

> And the servants of the Gracious God are those who walk on the earth in a dignified manner, and when the ignorant address them, they say, 'Peace!'

77. Al-Furqān, 25:64

> Ḥaḍrat Abū Sa'īd Khudrī[ra] narrates that the Holy Prophet[sa] said, 'Anyone who adopts a degree of humility, Allah will elevate his status to a degree so much so that he will be granted a place in *'Il-liyyīn* [*i.e., the highest of the high*]. And the one who shows arrogance in front of Allah and adopts a degree of vanity, Allah will lower his spiritual status to such a degree so much so that He will make him reach *Asfal-us-Sāfilīn* [the lowest of the low].' (*Musnadu Aḥmadabni Ḥanbal*, Bāqī Musnadil Mukthirīna minaṣ-Ṣaḥābah)

Your safety is to leave the company of such persons by saying '*salām*' to them. It is better for you because your spiritual levels will be raised, and the opponents will be falling among the lowest of the low.

Again, it is narrated in *ḥadīth*:

> Ḥaḍrat Abū Hurairah[ra] narrated that the Holy Prophet[sa] said, 'Your wealth does not decrease by giving *ṣadaqah* [charity]. And the more a person forgives others, the more Allah grants him honour; the more a person adopts humility and humbleness, the more Allah raises his status.' (*Ṣaḥīḥ Muslim*, Kitāb-ul-Birri waṣ-Ṣilah, Bābu Istiḥbābil 'Afwi Wat-Tawāḍu'i)

> 'Iyāḍ Bin Ḥimār al-Mujāshi'ī[ra] narrated that the Holy Prophet[sa] said, 'Allah has revealed to me that you should adopt humbleness to the extent that no one shows his pride to the others and no one commits any act of aggression against another.' (*Ṣaḥīḥ Muslim,* Kitāb-ul-Jannati waṣ-Ṣifati Na'īmihā Wa Ahlihā, Bābuṣ-Sifātillatī yo'arafu bihā fid-Dunyā Ahlul-Jannati Wa Ahlun-Nār)

There is another tradition we should also keep in mind as with respect to mutual matters and dealings.

> Ḥaḍrat Abū Hurairah[ra] narrates that the Holy Prophet[sa] said, 'Wealth does not decrease when it is spent in the way of Allah, and the extent to which a servant of God forgives another, Allah the Almighty increases his honour likewise. The more humility and humbleness one adopts, the greater is the status one is granted by Allah the Almighty.' (*Ṣaḥīḥ Muslim,* Kitāb-ul-Birri waṣ-Ṣilah, Bābu Istiḥbābil 'Afwi Wat-Tawāḍu'i)

So each Aḥmadī should adopt the habit of forgiving each other. This would elevate one's status in the Hereafter, and Allah the Almighty shall continue to increase one's honour in this world as well. Allah the Almighty does not leave anything that is done for His cause without a reward.

Status of the Meek in the Eyes of the Holy Prophet Muḥammad[sa]

How great was the status of the meek in the eyes of the Holy Prophet[sa] might be determined by this *ḥadīth*:

> Ḥaḍrat Abū Sa'īd Khudrī[ra] narrates with reference to the Holy Prophet[sa] that he loved the meek. Ḥaḍrat Abū Sa'īd Khudrī[ra] said that he heard the Holy Prophet[sa] praying:

اَللّٰهُمَّ اَحْيِنِىْ مِسْكِيْنًا وَاَمِتْنِىْ مِسْكِيْنًا وَاحْشُرْنِىْ فِى زُمْرَةِ الْمَسَاكِيْن ـ

> O Allah keep me alive in a state of meekness, give me death in a state of meekness, and raise me from among the group of the meek.

(*Sunano Ibn-e-Mājah*, Kitābūz-Zuhd, Bābu Mujālasatil-Fuqarā'i)

Thus, each Aḥmadī should adopt the same path and should tread the ways on which our master the Holy Prophet[sa] was. Each Aḥmadī should try and be counted among the meek, for the pledge of *bai'at* states that, 'I shall spend my life in meekness.'

It is narrated in one tradition:

> Ḥaḍrat Abū Hurairah[ra] narrates that, 'Ḥaḍrat Ja'far[ra] Bin Abī Ṭālib used to love the meek and needy. He would sit in their gatherings and would talk to them, and the meek and needy would talk to him. Therefore, the Holy Prophet[sa] would call Ḥaḍrat Ja'far[ra] with the title of *'Abūl Masākīn* [i.e., the father of the meek].' (*Sunano Ibn-e-Mājah*, Kitābūz-Zuhd, Bābu Mujālasatil-Fuqarā'i)

The Promised Messiah[as] says:

> If you wish to find Allah the Almighty, seek Him near the hearts of the meek. This is the reason Prophets of God adopted meekness. Similarly, it is required that people of bigger nations do not deride smaller nations; none should say their ancestry is higher. Allah the Almighty states that when you come before Me I shall not enquire of you about your nation; rather, the question would be, what are your deeds? Likewise, the Prophet[sa] of God said to his daughter that 'O Fāṭimah, Allah the Almighty shall not enquire into one's lineage. If you commit a wrong Allah the Almighty shall not condone you because you are the daughter of the Prophet.

> Thus, you should watch what you do at all times. (*Malfūẓāt*, new ed., vol. 3, p. 370)

He also states:

> It was an essential requirement for *ahl-e-taqwā* [righteous people] that they spend their life in poverty and meekness. This is a branch of *taqwā* by which we are to ward off the unjustified anger. The last and most crucial stage for great pious and honest people is indeed to shun anger. Haughtiness and conceit are borne out of anger, and similarly, anger is at times a consequence of haughtiness and conceit. Anger is aroused only when man gives preference to one's *nafs* [self] over the other. (*Report Jalsah Sālānah*, 1897, p. 49)

He states:

> If you wish that God in heaven is pleased with you, then be as if you are two brothers from one womb. The more esteemed among you is one who forgives the sins of his brother, and wretched is one who is obstinate and does not forgive. Such a person is not from me. (*Kashti-e-Nūḥ, Rūḥānī Khazā'in*, vol. 19, p. 12–13)

CONDITION VIII

That he/she shall hold faith, the honour of faith and the cause of Islām dearer to his/her life than wealth, honour, children, and all loved ones.

The pledge to prefer faith over the world is a pledge that everyone who is constantly linked with the Jamā'at and attends meetings and *ijtimā'āt* repeats over and over again. Banners are set up at every *ijtimā'*, *jalsah*, etc. Often, one of these banners displays the idea of giving preference to faith over the world. Why has this matter been given so much importance? Without it, faith cannot survive. It is not an easy task to act upon this requirement. To achieve it, one should constantly ask for Allah's help. This high standard can only be established with His grace. For us who are (with the grace of Allah) in *bai'at* of the Promised Messiah[as], Allah the Almighty has given the instruction in the Holy Qur'ān:[78]

وَمَآ اُمِرُوْٓا اِلَّا لِيَعْبُدُوا اللّٰهَ مُخْلِصِيْنَ لَهُ الدِّيْنَ ۔ حُنَفَآءَ وَيُقِيْمُوا الصَّلٰوةَ
وَيُؤْتُوا الزَّكٰوةَ وَذٰلِكَ دِيْنُ الْقَيِّمَةِ

> And they were not commanded but to serve Allah, being sincere to Him in obedience, *and* being upright, and to observe Prayer, and pay the *Zakāt*. And that is the religion *of the people* of the right path…

By offering *Ṣalāt* on time and in congregation, and by spending in the cause of Allah and helping the needy, we can establish ourselves upon the correct religion. Thus, we can incorporate the teachings into our lives and enforce them in our conduct; and when we worship Allah and act upon His teachings, Allah the Almighty will give us the ability to do so. He will strengthen our faith to such an extent that our selves, our ambitions, and our children will all appear insignificant in comparison to our faith. So, when everything will be purely for Allah the Almighty, and nothing will be considered our own possession, then Allah will not let us go to waste. He guards the honour, protects the children, and puts His blessings on such people. He enlarges their possessions, always keeps them wrapped in His Mercy and Favour, and removes all their fears. As Allah says in the Holy Qur'ān:[79]

بَلٰى مَنْ اَسْلَمَ وَجْهَهٗ لِلّٰهِ وَهُوَ مُحْسِنٌ فَلَهٗٓ اَجْرُهٗ عِنْدَ رَبِّهٖ وَلَا خَوْفٌ عَلَيْهِمْ
وَلَا هُمْ يَحْزَنُوْنَ

> Nay, whoever submits himself completely to Allah, while he is excellent in conduct, shall have his reward with his Lord. No fear *shall come* upon such, neither shall they grieve.

78. Al-Bayyinah, 98:6
79. Al-Baqarah, 2:113

Essence of Islāmic Teachings

Then Allah says:[80]

وَمَنْ اَحْسَنُ دِيْنًا مِّمَّنْ اَسْلَمَ وَجْهَهٗ لِلّٰهِ وَهُوَ مُحْسِنٌ وَّاتَّبَعَ مِلَّةَ اِبْرَاهِيْمَ حَنِيْفًا. وَاتَّخَذَ اللّٰهُ اِبْرَاهِيْمَ خَلِيْلًا

And who is better in faith than he who submits himself to Allah, and he is a doer of good, and follows the religion of Abraham, the upright? And Allah took Abraham for a special friend.

In this verse, the essence of teachings of Islām is recorded. One should be completely obedient and should follow the commands of Allah with all his strengths. He should dedicate himself to faith and be gracious. One should not fear that his wealth or children would be wasted. Allah, who is better than anyone else in returning favours and in rewarding efforts, will reward these actions Himself. As has been explained earlier, He Himself will protect his life, wealth, and honour. Allah the Almighty does not let such people or their future generations go to waste.

Referencing the Qur'ān, the Promised Messiah[as] says:[81]

بَلٰى مَنْ اَسْلَمَ وَجْهَهٗ لِلّٰهِ وَهُوَ مُحْسِنٌ فَلَهٗ اَجْرُهٗ عِنْدَ رَبِّهٖ وَلَاخَوْفٌ عَلَيْهِمْ وَلَا هُمْ يَحْزَنُوْنَ

Whoever submits before God, dedicates his life in His path, and is eager to do righteous deeds shall get his rewards from

80. Al-Nisā', 4:126
81. Al-Baqarah, 2:113

> the fountainhead of nearness to God. There is neither fear nor grief on such people. Whoever devotes all his faculties to the path of God, and whoever is active doing truly righteous deeds with his words, conduct, movements, standing, and his entire life is purely for the sake of God, will have a special reward. God will deliver him from fear and grief. (*Sirāj-ud-Dīn 'Īsā'ī ke Chār Swāloṅ kā Jawāb, Rūḥānī Khazā'in*, vol. 12, p. 344)

It is narrated in a tradition:

> Ḥaḍrat Mu'āwiyah Bin Ḥaidah al-Qushairī[ra] says while narrating the story of his acceptance of Islām, 'I reached the Holy Prophet[sa] and I asked him, "What message has our Lord given you for us, and what religion have you brought?" He said, "God has sent me with the religion of Islām." I asked, "What is the religion of Islām?" Ḥuḍūr[sa] replied, "Islām is that you surrender your entire being to Allah, abandon all other deities, establish *Ṣalāt*, and give *Zakāt*."' (*Al-Istī'āb*)

There is another tradition:

> Ḥaḍrat Sufyān[ra] says that once I said, 'O Messenger of Allah, tell me something of Islām after which I will not have to ask anyone else and I should be fully satisfied.' Ḥuḍūr[sa] replied, 'You should say: "I believe in Allah the Almighty, then become firm on it, and stay on it with fortitude."' (*Ṣaḥīḥ Muslim,* Kitāb-ul-Īmān, Bābu Jāmi'i Auṣāfil-Islām)

What was the conduct of the Companions[ra]? The following incident is recorded in *ḥadīth*. In the beginning, alcohol was not forbidden in Islām. Companions[ra] would drink and sometimes get intoxicated. But even in this state, faith and its honour were dominant in their minds. They placed faith as more important than all other things. When the commandment prohibiting alcohol came, some people were sitting together drinking and some were intoxicated. When they heard of the prohibition, they acted upon it immediately.

> Ḥaḍrat Anas Bin Mālīk[ra] narrates, 'I was serving wine prepared from dates to Abū Ṭalḥah Anṣārī[ra], Abū 'Ubaidah Bin Jarrāḥ[ra] and Ubayy Bin Ka'ab[ra]. Someone came and said alcohol has been forbidden, and when Abū Ṭalḥah[ra] heard this he said to Anas[ra], "Get up and break the containers of wine." Anas[ra] adds that he got up and hit the containers with the bottom of the stone vase and it broke them.' (*Ṣaḥīḥ Al-Bukhārī*, Kitābu Khabaril-Wāḥidi, Bābu mā Jā'a fī Ijāzatil-Wāḥidiṣ-Ṣuḍūq)

Revival of Islām Demands a Ransom from Us

The Promised Messiah[as] says:

> Revival of Islām demands a ransom from us. What is it? It is us dying in this very path. This is the death upon which the life of Islām, the life of Muslims, and the manifestation of the Living God depend. This is exactly what is called Islām, and God now wants to revive this very Islām. To bring about this great undertaking, it is essential that a grand enterprise that would be effective in every aspect should be established by His own initiative. So, the Wise and Powerful God did exactly that by sending this humble one for the reformation of mankind. (*Fat-ḥe-Islām, Rūḥānī Khazā'in*, vol. 3, p. 10–12)

Then he says:

> Until man becomes a servant of Allah with sincerity and purity, it is hard to attain any rank. Allah the Almighty testifies about Ibrāhīm:[82]
>
> وَاِبْرَاهِيْمَ الَّذِىْ وَفّٰى
>
> That Ibrāhīm is a man who lived up to his word. To cleanse one's heart in this manner, to fill it up with the love of Allah, to live according to the wishes of Allah, and to be an obedient servant whose desires are in perfect harmony with the desires of Allah, like a shadow. All of these things are achieved with prayer. *Ṣalāt* is for praying indeed, and one should pray at every stage. But if one offers the *ṣalāt* as if he were asleep, and does not know [the nature and importance of] *Ṣalāt*, then it is not *Ṣalāt* at all.... Therefore, it is required that man should not be lazy in offering the *Ṣalāt*, nor should he be inattentive. If our Community wishes to become a Jamā'at, it should adopt a type of death. It should avoid selfish matters and selfish motives, and it should give Allah the Almighty priority over everything. (*Malfūẓāt*, new ed., vol. 3, p. 457–458)

82. And of Abraham who fulfilled *the commandments*. Al-Najm, 53:38

Means of Obtaining Salvation From Sin—Certainty of Faith

Then the Promised Messiah[as] says:

> O ye, the seekers of God: pay attention and listen. There is nothing like certainty of faith. Certainty rescues one from sin. Certainty gives one strength to do good. Certainty makes one a true lover of Allah. Can one give up sin without certainty? Can one desist from the desires of the flesh without convincing manifestation? Can one find any satisfaction without certainty? Can one bring about a true change without certainty? Can one achieve true happiness without certainty? Is there any such penance or ransom that can make one give up sin?... One should remember that without certainty, one cannot come out of a dark life, nor can one be able to attain the Holy Spirit. Blessed are those who have been delivered from doubts and misgivings because they alone will be delivered from sin. Blessed are those who have escaped uncertainty and doubt because they will get rid of sin. Blessed are you when you are given the treasure of certainty because after that your sin will disappear. Sin and certainty cannot co-exist. Would one put his hand in a hole in which he could see a poisonous snake? Can one stand at the place where stones rain from a volcano, or where lightening strikes, or at the place of attack of a vicious lion, or at a place where a deadly plague is wiping out the human race? If you have this much certainty about God as about the snake, or the lightening, or the lion, or the plague, then it is not possible for you to defy

> Him nor to break the ties of sincerity and loyalty with Him. (*Kashti-e-Nūḥ, Rūḥānī Khazā'in*, vol. 19, p. 66–67)

The Promised Messiah[as] also said:

> Perfect understanding is the root of fear, love and appreciation. Whoever is given the prefect knowledge is given the perfection of fear and love as well. Whoever is given perfect fear and love is given freedom from every sin that originates from recklessness. For this salvation, we are not dependent on any blood, we are not in need of any cross, and we do not need any penance. Instead, we only need one sacrifice, the sacrifice of the 'self'. Its need is felt by our conscience, and this sacrifice is named Islām. Islām entails putting out your own neck for sacrifice. It means to put your soul on the threshold of God with total willingness. This charming name is the soul of all revealed laws and the crux of all commandments. To put out one's neck to be sacrificed with real pleasure and contentment requires perfect love and perfect devotion. Perfect love requires perfect understanding. Thus, the word Islām points to the fact that true sacrifice needs perfect understanding and perfect love. And it needs nothing else. (*Lecture Lahore, Rūḥānī Khazā'in*, vol. 20, p. 151–152)

May Allah the Almighty grant us the ability to act upon all these exhortations.

[From the Friday sermon delivered at the Faḍl Mosque, London, United Kingdom, on September 12, 2003, in which ninth condition of bai'at was discussed in detail.]

The teachings of Islām are so beautiful that they have not left any aspect of human life untouched. All of these favours of Allah the Almighty demand that this teaching, which descended on His dear Prophet[sa], be adopted as part of our lives. We bear even greater responsibility as we have joined and claimed to have joined the Jamā'at of the true lover and servant of the Holy Prophet[sa], and the *Imām* of this age. Thus, whereas Allah the Almighty has drawn attention towards His worship and the discharge of one's obligations toward Him, He has also drawn the attention toward the discharge of our obligations to humans. He has also commanded us regarding the rights of different relatives and relationships that need to be discharged. It is due to this importance that the Promised Messiah[as] mentioned in the ninth condition of *bai'at* kindness towards the creation of Allah the Almighty and the obligations owed to them.

CONDITION IX

That he/she shall keep himself/herself occupied in the service of God's creatures for His sake only and shall endeavour towards the beneficence of mankind to the best of his/her God-given abilities and powers.

Allah the Almighty says in the Holy Qur'ān:[83]

وَاعْبُدُوا اللّٰهَ وَلَاتُشْرِكُوْا بِهٖ شَيْئًا وَّبِالْوَالِدَيْنِ اِحْسَانًا وَّ بِذِى الْقُرْبٰى وَالْيَتٰمٰى وَالْمَسٰكِيْنِ وَالْجَارِذِى الْقُرْبٰى وَالْجَارِالْجُنُبِ وَالصَّاحِبِ بِالْجَنْبِ وَابْنِ السَّبِيْلِ وَمَامَلَكَتْ اَيْمَانُكُمْ اِنَّ اللّٰهَ لَايُحِبُّ مَنْ كَانَ مُخْتَالًا فَخُوْرًا

And worship Allah and associate naught with Him, and *show* kindness to parents, and to kindred, and orphans, and the needy, and to the neighbour that is a kinsman and the neighbour that is a stranger, and the companion by *your* side, and the

83. Al-Nisā', 4:37

wayfarer, and those whom your right hands possess. Surely, Allah loves not the proud *and* the boastful.

Kind Treatment to All

In this verse, Allah the Almighty commands not only to treat your brothers, your near ones, your relatives, your acquaintances, and your neighbors kindly, but also be compassionate to them, help them if they are in need, and be beneficent to the best of your ability to even those people whom you do not know and have no relationship or association with. And be beneficent to those whom you have only met temporarily. If they are in need of your sympathy or your help and can benefit from you, then you must help them. By doing so, a beautiful culture of Islām will be established. Develop compassion for God's creatures, with the understanding that it is something more than a good deed, it falls into the category of benevolence. Benevolence means not expecting the return of your favours; benevolence is exercised by man purely for the sake of Allah the Almighty. In this way, such a beautiful society will be established where there will be no dispute between husband and wife, mother-in-law and daughter-in-law, brothers, and neighbors. Everyone will try to be benevolent to the other. Each person will try to give others their rights with love and care, and will do so purely to win the love of Allah. In today's society, this is even more urgent than ever before. Allah says that if you do not follow this path, then you will be counted as arrogant. And Allah does not like arrogance.

Arrogance is such an affliction that all mischief originates from it.... In the seventh condition, I have mentioned the subject in depth already; therefore, it is not necessary to go into another detailed discussion about it. Briefly, this condition requires you to be kind to God's creation so that you may become favourable in the sight of Allah the Almighty and get the rewards in both the worlds. The kindness you show towards others should be motivated by heart-felt love and not to seek acknowledgement from people for the favour. Allah says in the Holy Qur'ān:[84]

وَيُطْعِمُوْنَ الطَّعَامَ عَلٰى حُبِّهٖ مِسْكِيْنًا وَّيَتِيْمًا وَّ اَسِيْرًا

And they feed, for love of Him, the poor, the orphan, and the prisoner.

One interpretation of this is that despite their own needs, those who love Allah take care of the needs of others in order to attain the love of Allah the Almighty. They themselves stay hungry, yet they feed others. They do not show miserliness by suggesting that what they are giving is also required to meet their own needs. Instead, they help as much as they can. They do this to be virtuous and to get the approval of Allah the Almighty, and not to get any acknowledgement from others. They give what they could enjoy or utilize themselves, always keeping in mind the instruction of Allah that you should only give for the sake of Allah, what you like for yourself. They are not like those who help the needy and boast about it. Some people are in the habit of giving only their used items or

84. Al-Dahr, 76:9

worn clothing as gifts. These people should respect the dignity of their brothers and sisters. It is better for them not to give a gift at all if they cannot afford it. At a minimum, they should tell the recipient that the items are used and then ask the recipient if they are willing to accept them.

Some people write to me saying that they want to give—for the weddings of poor girls—good clothes that have only been worn for a day or two and were not used again because they were too small or for some other reason. In this regard, it must be clear that even if these items are being given through the auxiliary organisations of Jamā'at-e-Aḥmadiyyah, like *Lajnah Imā'illāh* or *Khuddām-ul-Aḥmadiyyah*, or even if they are being given individually, they should respect the dignity of the poor. They should give away items in a condition that they are still worth giving. The items should not be completely worn out with stains, stench of sweat, etc. If such clothes are given, they should be washed, cleaned, and mended first. As I have said, our auxiliary organisations like *Lajnah Imā'illāh* also distribute such clothes. They should make it clear to the recipients that these clothes are used and that they should only accept them if they choose to. Everyone has a sense of honour, and as I have said earlier, this sense of honour should be respected.

The Promised Messiah[as] says in explaining the verse:[85]

وَيُطْعِمُوْنَ الطَّعَامَ عَلٰى حُبِّهٖ مِسْكِيْنًا وَّيَتِيْمًا وَّ اَسِيْرًا

...Remember that God the Almighty likes good deeds very much, and He desires that sympathy be shown for His

85. Al-Dahr, 76:9

creation. If He desired harm, He would have directed us to be bad; but the Majesty of God is free from this. (Holy is Allah and Great is His station)…

Therefore, all of you who have established a relationship with me should remember that you should show compassion for everyone regardless of their religion; and be good to all without any discrimination because this is the teaching of Holy Qur'ān:[86]

وَيُطْعِمُوْنَ الطَّعَامَ عَلٰى حُبِّهٖ مِسْكِيْنًا وَّيَتِيْمًا وَّ اَسِيْرًا

Those captives and prisoners [at the time of the Prophet] were mostly non-believers. Now, you can see the scope of kindness in Islām. In my opinion, perfect moral teaching is not found anywhere except in Islām. Once I regain my health, I will *inshā' Allah* write a comprehensive treatise on moral teachings because I want to make my expectations clear to the Jamā'at. It will be a comprehensive guide for my Jamā'at, and it should show how to seek God's pleasure. I am deeply grieved when I see or hear that someone did something that does not fully conform to Islāmic teachings. I am not happy about these incidents. I still view my Jamā'at like a child who takes two steps and falls four times. But I do believe that Allah the Almighty will make it perfect. Therefore, you should make an effort, plan, strive, and pray continuously that Allah may show His grace, because nothing is possible without His grace. When He favours, He opens up all ways. (*Malfūẓāt*, new ed., vol. 4, p. 218–219)

86. Al-Dahr, 76:9

With the Grace of Allah, due to the pious influence of the Promised Messiah[as], and by acting on his teachings, many of the ills that the Promised Messiah[as] was concerned about [regarding the Jamā'at] at that time disappeared from the Jamā'at. With the Grace of Allah, a very large segment was totally freed from them, and it still is. As we are moving away from that stage, Satan continues to attack with the ills of society. Therefore, in accordance with the concerns of the Promised Messiah[as], we should continue to strive to avoid those ills with effort and prayer. We should ask for the Grace of Allah in accordance with his teaching, so that Allah the Almighty may always keep the Jamā'at of Promised Messiah[as] perfect. I will now present a few traditions.

> Ḥaḍrat Abū Hurairah[ra] narrates that the Messenger of Allah said, 'Allah the Almighty and the Glorious will say on the Day of Judgement, "O son of Adam, I was sick but you did not attend to Me." Man will say, "O Lord. How could I attend to You? You are the Lord of all the worlds." Allah the Almighty will say, "Did you not know that so and so of My servants was sick? You did not attend to him. Did you not know that if you had done so, you would have found Me near him? O son of Adam, I asked you for food but you did not give Me any food." Upon this the son of Adam will say, "O my Lord. How could I feed You whereas You are the Lord of all the worlds?" Allah the Almighty will say, "Do you not remember when a servant of Mine asked you for food? You did not feed him. Did you not know that if you had fed him, you would have had a reward with Me? O son of Adam! I asked you for water, but you did not give Me any water." Son of Adam will say, "O

my Lord. How could I serve you water, whereas You are the Lord of all the worlds?" Upon this, Allah the Almighty will say, "Such and such person asked you for some water, but you did not offer him any. If you had given him water, you would have had its reward with Me.'" (*Ṣaḥīḥ Muslim,* Kitāb-ul-Birri waṣ-Ṣilah, Bābu Faḍli 'Iyādatil-Marīḍ)

Then, there is this narration:

Ḥaḍrat 'Abdūllah Bin Mas'ūd[ra] states that the Messenger of Allah said, 'All creatures are God's family. So, Allah likes the person, from among all humans, who treats His family (creatures) well and looks after their needs.' (*Mishkāt-ul-Maṣābīḥ*, Bābush-Shafaqati war-Raḥmati 'alal-Khalq)

There is another *ḥadīth* in which Ḥaḍrat 'Alī[ra] narrates that the Messenger of Allah said:

'Every Muslim has six obligations with regard to other Muslims:

1. When he meets him, he should say '*Assalāmo 'Alaikum*.'
2. When one sneezes, he should say, '*Yarḥamukallāh*' [may Allah have mercy on you].
3. When he is sick, he should visit him. Some people have, with the grace of Allah, this good habit, and they go to hospitals to visit sick ones whether they know them or not. They take fruits and flowers for them. This form of social service is very good.
4. When one calls him for help, he responds to him.
5. When one dies, he comes to his funeral.

6. And he desires for them what he desires for himself, and even in his absence he wishes him well.'

(*Sunanud-Dārimiyyi*, Kitāb-ul-Istīdhān, Bābun fī Ḥaqqil-Muslimi 'alal-Muslim)

It is reported that:

Ḥaḍrat 'Abdullāh Bin 'Umar[ra] narrates that the Messenger of Allah said, 'Do not be jealous of one another. Do not raise prices to harm each other. Do not hold grudges against each other. Do not turn your backs on each other, and do not be indifferent to each other. And do not bid on deals that are closed. Instead, you should live like servants of God and be brotherly to each other. A Muslim does not wrong his brother. He does not insult him, and he does not embarrass or humiliate him." He pointed to his chest and said, "Piety is here." He repeated these words three times, then he said, "It is enough misfortune for a man that he should look at his Muslim brother with disdain. Every Muslim's blood, wealth, honour and respect are sacred and sanctified for the other Muslim.' (*Ṣaḥīḥ Muslim,* Kitāb-ul-Birri waṣ-Ṣilah, Bābu Taḥrīmī-Ẓulmil Muslimī Wa Khadhlih)

Then it is reported that:

Ḥaḍrat Abū Hurairah[ra] states that the Holy Prophet[sa] said, 'Whosoever helps remove the worldly anguish and suffering of a Muslim will have his anguish and suffering removed by Allah the Almighty on the Day of Judgement. Whosoever brings relief to a poor person and brings ease to him will have ease created for him by Allah in the hereafter. Whosoever covers

> up the faults of a Muslim will have his faults covered up by Allah the Almighty in the hereafter. Allah the Almighty is keen to help him who is keen to help his brother. Whosoever goes in search of knowledge will have the ways to Paradise facilitated to him by Allah the Almighty. Those who sit in any of the houses of Allah and read the Book of Allah and are engaged in teaching and learning will attain peace and tranquillity from Allah the Almighty; Allah's mercy covers them, angels keep them in their circle, and Allah the Almighty mentions them to His near ones. One who slackens in actions will not succeed with only his name and his family, and he will not go to Paradise by virtue of his family ties.' (*Ṣaḥīḥ Muslim,* Kitāb-udh-Dhikr, Bābu Faḍlil Ijtimā'i 'alā Tilāwatil-Qur'ānī wa 'aladh-Dhikr)

What is mentioned in the beginning is to be mindful of the rights of other people and help to remove the worries and difficulties of your brethren. If you do so, on the Day of Judgement, Allah the Almighty will deal with you with the same kindness and will remove your worries and hardships. It is the favour of the Holy Prophet[sa] upon us. He said that if you wish that Allah should cover you with His forgiveness, then you should help and comfort the distressed, the afflicted, and the destitute as much as you can. Then, Allah will deal with you with kindness. Try to cover the weaknesses of your brethren. Do not try to find their faults or make them public. You do not know how many weaknesses and faults you have that you will have to account for on the Day of Judgement. Thus, if you had overlooked the faults of your brethren, if you had tried to counsel them with sympathy instead of making their weaknesses public, Allah will overlook your faults as well. These are the rights of people. If you discharge them, you will inherit the blessings of Allah the Almighty.

Then it is reported in a tradition that:

> Ḥaḍrat Abū Hurairah[ra] narrates that the Holy Prophet[sa] said, 'Charity does not reduce your wealth. The person who forgives the transgressions of others will be given even greater honour by Allah the Almighty. No one is dishonoured by forgiving the faults of others.' (*Musnadu Aḥmadabni Ḥanbal*, vol. 2. p. 235, printed in Beirut)

Then it is reported that:

> Ḥaḍrat 'Abdullāh Bin 'Umar[ra] states that the Holy Prophet[sa] said, 'The Gracious God will be Merciful to those who show mercy to others. You show mercy to the dwellers of the earth, and the One in the heavens will have mercy on you.' (*Sunano Abī Dāwūd*, Kitāb-ul-Adab, Bābun fir-Raḥmah)

The Promised Messiah[as] says:

> Remember that there are two commandments of Allah the Almighty. First, associate no partner with Him, neither in His being and attributes, nor in His worship. Second, be compassionate to the others. Benevolence does not imply that it should be only for your brothers and relations, but it should be for anyone, any human, and any of God's creation. Do not consider whether someone is a Hindu or a Christian. I tell you truthfully that Allah the Almighty has taken the responsibility of ensuring justice to you; He does not want you to take it upon yourselves. The more congeniality you adopt, the

more humble and serving you are, the more Allah the Almighty will be pleased with you. Leave your enemies to Allah the Almighty. The Day of Judgement is near. You should not be confounded by the opposition. I perceive that you will suffer a lot more at their hands because those who fall short of decency become ferocious as if a dam is broken and a flood bursts out. A pious person needs to control his tongue. (*Malfūẓāt*, vol. 9, p. 164–165)

Then he says:

Beware there are two categories of rights. One is Allah's right and the second is the human right. Even in connection with the right of Allah, the affluent encounter difficulty, and arrogance and conceit keep them deprived. For example, they dislike standing next to a poor person in Prayer. They cannot have him sit next to them, and thus they remain deficient in matters of Allah's right. Mosques are indeed the houses for the poor, and these people consider it below their stature to go there. Similarly, they cannot take part in special activities in connection with the rights of man. A poor man is prepared for any service. He can massage your feet, bring water, wash clothes and does not hesitate if he has to help remove the human refuse. But the rich consider such tasks to be insulting and disgraceful and are thus deprived of these blessings as well. Thus, prosperity can also stop you from doing a number of virtuous deeds. This is why it is reported in traditions that the poor will enter Paradise five hundred years earlier. (*Malfūẓāt* new ed., vol. 3, p. 368)

He also says:

> Compassion for God's creation is such a thing that if man gives it up and moves away from it, he gradually becomes a beast. This is what the humanity of man demands, and one is human only as long as one treats one's brother with kindness, tenderness, and benevolence. There should be no discrimination in this matter. Just as Sa'dī said, 'human beings are like parts of a body.' Remember, in my estimation the scope of sympathy is very wide. One should not exclude any group or individual. I do not say—like the ignorant people of this age—that you should limit your kindness to only Muslims. I say that you should have sympathy for all of God's creation no matter who they are, whether a Hindu, or a Muslim, or something else. I never approve the words of such people who wish to limit sympathy only to their own people. (*Malfūẓāt*, new ed., vol. 4, p. 216–217)

He also says:

> Thus, to be kind to the human race and have compassion for it is a very great type of worship and it is a great way to win the pleasure of Allah the Almighty; but I see a great deficiency is shown in this regard. Others are considered inferior. They are mocked at instead of being looked after and helped in a time of calamity and distress. Those who do not treat the poor well, even consider them inferior, I fear they may get afflicted by the same calamity. Those whom Allah has blessed should express their gratitude and should deal with His creation kindly and humanely. They should not be proud of God-

given abundance, and they should not viciously trample the poor. (*Malfūẓāt*, new ed., vol. 4, p. 438–439)

He also says:

> The great details about the rights of parents, children, other relatives, and the destitute as described in the Qur'ān are not, in my estimation, written in any other book.
>
> As Allah the Almighty says:[87]
>
> وَاعْبُدُوا اللّٰهَ وَلَا تُشْرِكُوْا بِهٖ شَيْئًا وَّبِالْوَالِدَيْنِ اِحْسَانًا وَّ بِذِى الْقُرْبٰى وَالْيَتٰمٰى وَالْمَسٰكِيْنِ وَالْجَارِ ذِى الْقُرْبٰى وَالْجَارِ الْجُنُبِ وَالصَّاحِبِ بِالْجَنْبِ وَابْنِ السَّبِيْلِ وَمَا مَلَكَتْ اَيْمَانُكُمْ اِنَّ اللّٰهَ لَا يُحِبُّ مَنْ كَانَ مُخْتَالًا فَخُوْرًا
>
> And worship Allah and associate naught with Him, and *show* kindness to parents, and to kindred, and orphans, and the needy, and to the neighbour that is a kinsman and the neighbour that is a stranger, and the companion by *your* side, and the wayfarer, and those whom your right hands possess. Surely, Allah loves not the proud *and* the boastful.
>
> (*Chashmah-e-Ma'rifat*, *Rūḥānī Khazā'in*, vol. 23, p. 208–209)

Ḥaḍrat Khalīfatul Masīḥ I[ra] says in this regard:

> The intention should be in accord with the verse:[88]
>
> اِنَّا نَخَافُ مِنْ رَّبِّنَا يَوْمًا عَبُوْسًا قَمْطَرِيْرًا

87. Al-Nisā', 4:37
88. Al-Dahr, 76:11

...Verily, we fear our Lord, and the day that is: '*Abūs* and *Qamṭarīr.*

'*Abūs* is hardship, constraint, and straitness. And *Qamṭarīr* is prolonged. It states that day of Day of Judgement will be hard and long.

By virtue of feeding the hungry, Allah the Almighty will also safeguard one from the intensity and duration of suffering during a famine. As a result:[89]

فَوَقٰهُمُ اللّٰهُ شَرَّ ذٰلِکَ الْیَوْمِ وَلَقّٰهُمْ نَضْرَةً وَّسُرُوْرًا

God Almighty protects one from the evil of this day, and this protection is due to one's cheerfulness and happiness.

I say once again: remember helping the poor and the needy in this day and age and it will save you from the difficulties of the Judgement Day. May God Almighty grant you and me the opportunity to strive for attaining the respect and pleasure of the Everlasting, *Āmīn.*

(*Ḥaqā'iq-ul-Furqān*, vol. 4, p. 290–291)

This is a distinction for Aḥmadiyyah Muslim Jamā'at that it takes part in social welfare activities as much as it has the capacity for with the resources available to it. It does as much as it possibly can for the in service of people and humanity, staying within its means, both as individuals and as the Jamā'at. The members of the Jamā'at help to fight hunger, treat the poor, help in education and in the marriages of the

89. So Allah will save them from the evil of that day, and will grant them cheerfulness and happiness. Al-Dahr, 76:12

poor by joining in aid programs under the auspices of the Jamā'at. This fulfils their pledge of *bai'at* as they should.

May we never become like those nations and countries, which destroy their excess crops rather than help the suffering humanity because they see no political purpose or advantage in helping them. They think that poor people do not accept all their directives and dictates. Such people are kept starved and deprived as a punishment. May Allah enable Aḥmadiyyah Muslim Jamā'at to serve humanity even more then ever before.

At this time, I want to say that this service to humanity is being performed at the Jamā'at level according to its capacity. The sincere members of the Jamā'at are given the ability by Allah the Almighty to serve humanity. They give large sums of money with which service to humanity is provided. With the grace of Allah, there are doctors and teachers who have dedicated their lives and are serving in Africa, Rabwah, and in Qādiān as well. I appeal to every Aḥmadī doctor, every Aḥmadī teacher, every Aḥmadī lawyer, and every Aḥmadī who by virtue of his profession can serve humanity in any way, to try to help the poor and the needy. As a reward, Allah the Almighty will increase your wealth and your lives even more. *Inshā' Allah*[90], if all of you will provide this service with the intention of fulfiling a pledge to the *Imām* of the age, then you will see, *inshā' Allah*, there will be such a rain of God's blessings and favours that you will not be able to contain them.

90. An Arabic term meaning 'God-willing'.

The Promised Messiah[as] and His Concern for Humanity

The Promised Messiah's[as] advice on kindness to humanity, particularly the kindness and help for your brethren, was explained on one occasion:

> My condition is that if someone is in pain and his cry reaches me, even if I am in Prayer I feel like breaking my Prayer so that I may help him if he can benefit from it. I should show compassion to him as much I am capable. This is against good morals that one should not assist his brother in distress or hardship. If you cannot do anything for him, you should at least pray for him. You should apply the same morals towards strangers and Hindus, not just your brethren, and you should show compassion to them all. One should never be careless and unconcerned.
>
> Once I was out walking and someone named 'Abdul Karīm was with me. He was a little ahead of me. Along the way, we met an old lady of seventy or seventy-five years. She gave him a letter to read for her, but he scolded her and pushed her aside, and it grieved me. She gave me the letter. I stopped and read it, and I explained it to her thoroughly. This embarrassed him, because he had to stop and wait anyway eventhough he was deprived of the reward. (*Malfūẓāt*, new ed., vol. 4, p. 82–83)

The Promised Messiah[as] also says:

> Be kind and merciful to humanity, for all are His creatures. Do not oppress them with your tongue, your hands, or in

> any other way. Always work for the good of mankind. Never unduly assert yourself with pride over others, even those who are placed under you. Never use abusive language for anyone, even if he abuses you. Be humble in spirit, kind, gentle, and forgiving, sympathetic towards all, and wish them well, so that you may be accepted.... If you are big, have mercy on those who are small and not contempt. If you are wise and well-versed in learning, serve the ignorant with words of wisdom. Never desire to bring disgrace on their lack of knowledge by trying to show off your own learning. If you are rich, instead of treating them with self-centred, disdainful pride, you should serve the poor. (*Kashti-e-Nūḥ, Rūḥānī Khazā'in*, vol. 19, p. 11–12)

Then he said:

> People will mistreat you and will hurt you in every way, but members of my Jamā'at should not be provoked. Do not use hurtful words in the heat of emotions. Allah the Almighty does not like such people. Allah the Almighty wants to make our Jamā'at exemplary.

He further says:

> Allah the Almighty loves the *muttaqī* [righteous]. You should always remain in awe of God's Majesty and be mindful that all are God's creatures. Do not persecute anyone, and do not have a quick temper or look at anyone with disdain. If there is one bad person in a Jamā'at, he can spoil others also. If your temper is inclined towards anger, then carefully examine the source of its fury. This aspect is very critical. (*Malfūẓāt*, new ed., vol. 1, p. 8–9)

He also says:

> Be such that your sincerity, loyalty, tenderness, and sensitivity should reach heaven. God protects such a person and gives him blessings when he sees that his heart is full of sincerity and loyalty. He sees your hearts and looks into them, not at your words and speech. If He finds the heart of a person to be pure and clean, He descends upon it and makes it His home. (*Malfūẓāt*, new ed., vol. 3, p. 181)

He also said:

> I repeat that those who are beneficial to mankind and are perfect in faith, sincerity, and loyalty will most certainly be saved. Therefore, you should try to develop these qualities in you. (*Malfūẓāt*, new ed., vol. 4, p. 184)

He also says:

> You cannot be accepted in the presence of the Lord unless you are pure, both on the outside and inside. If you are big, then have mercy on those who are small and not contempt. If you are wise and well-versed in learning, serve the ignorant with words of wisdom. Never desire to bring disgrace on their lack of knowledge by trying to show off your own learning. If you are rich, instead of treating them with self-centred, disdainful pride, you should serve the poor. Beware of the ways of destruction. Fear the Lord, and be righteous.... How unfortunate is the man who fails to believe in things coming from the mouth of God, which I have stated to you. If at all you desire that God in heaven be pleased with you, hasten to become one among yourselves as though you were brothers born of

> the same mother. Only he is the most honoured among you who most forgives the transgressions of his brother.... Unfortunate is he who remains obdurate and does not forgive. (*Kashti-e-Nūḥ, Rūḥānī Khazā'in*, vol. 19, p. 12–13)

He also said:

> To be compassionate towards God's creation is indeed a highly meritorious act, and Allah the Almighty likes it very much. What can be more valuable than showing compassion for such a person? Do you think that a master would be pleased with a friend if one of his servants went to his friend, but the friend did not take care of his servant? Never, even though the friend did not directly hurt the master. The kind treatment of his servant and hospitality shown to him amount to respecting the master. Similarly, God dislikes when someone ignores His creation, because He holds His creation dear. Thus, a person who shows kindness to His creation indeed pleases God. (*Malfūẓāt*, vol. 4, new ed., p. 215–216)

May Allah the Almighty give us the ability to act upon these admonishments of the Promised Messiah[as] and May he enable us to be true to the pledge that we have made with Him.

CONDITION X

That he/she shall enter into a bond of brotherhood with this humble servant of God, pledging obedience to me in everything good for the sake of God, and remain faithful to it until the day of his/her death. That he/she shall exert such a high devotion in the observance of this bond as is not to be found in any other worldly relationship and connection that demand devoted dutifulness.

[From the Friday sermon delivered at the Faḍl Mosque, London, United Kingdom, on September 19, 2003, in which tenth condition of bai'at was discussed in detail.]

In this condition, the Promised Messiah[as] is taking a pledge from us that by joining this organisation we are establishing a bond of brotherhood with him. Every Muslim is a brother of the other Muslim. But the relationship of love and brotherhood that is being established means much more than that. You are not merely establishing a bond of equals; instead, you are acknowledging that it is a command of Allah and His Messenger to accept the Messiah that was promised. Therefore, you are establishing this bond for the sake of Allah the Almighty. You are making this contract to uphold the religion of Allah the Almighty and to convey and spread the religion of Islām to all corners of the world. This bond can only be successful and long-lasting if you pledge to be obedient in everything good and keep this pledge until death. You should be mindful that this bond does not remain inactive, but should become stronger every day. It should be so strong and its standard should be so high that, in comparison, all other relations, bonds, and friendships should prove weaker. The bond should be so matchless and strong that in its comparison all other bonds and relations should seem meaningless.

Then he says that the thought can cross one's mind that in family relationships sometimes the rule of give and take—to compromise, to accept , and to have one's decisions accepted occasionally—is applicable. Here it must be understood that this, instead, is the bond of a slave and servant. Indeed, it should be even more than that. You have to be obedient without any grumbling. You never have the right to say that such and such cannot be done or that you cannot do such and such at this time. When you have taken the *bai'at* and have entered the organisation of the Jamā'at of the Promised Messiah[as], you have given everything of your's to the Promised Messiah[as]. You have to obey his decisions; you have to act upon his teachings. Since the system of *khilāfat* exists after him, you have to follow the decisions and the instructions of the *Khalīfah* of the time. Here you should not think that the servant or the subordinate has to obey because he is helpless and is obligated to serve. Servants sometimes grumble too. Always keep in mind that although your condition is that of a servant, it is really much higher because it is a bond of brotherhood and acknowledgement of obedience for the sake of Allah that comes with the pledge of sacrifice. The reward for sacrifice is received only if the sacrifice is offered with pleasure. This condition is such that the more one thinks about it, the deeper one submerges oneself in the love of the Promised Messiah[as] and the more one will find oneself bound by the organisation of the Jamā'at.

In the Noble Qur'ān, Allah the Almighty says:[91]

يٰاَيُّهَا النَّبِيُّ اِذَا جَآءَكَ الْمُؤْمِنٰتُ يُبَايِعْنَكَ عَلٰٓى اَنْ لَّا يُشْرِكْنَ بِاللّٰهِ شَيْئًا
وَّلَا يَسْرِقْنَ وَلَا يَزْنِيْنَ وَلَا يَقْتُلْنَ اَوْلَادَهُنَّ وَلَا يَاْتِيْنَ بِبُهْتَانٍ يَّفْتَرِيْنَهٗ بَيْنَ
اَيْدِيْهِنَّ وَاَرْجُلِهِنَّ وَلَا يَعْصِيْنَكَ فِيْ مَعْرُوْفٍ فَبَايِعْهُنَّ وَاسْتَغْفِرْلَهُنَّ اللّٰهَ.
اِنَّ اللّٰهَ غَفُوْرٌ رَّحِيْمٌ

O Prophet! When believing women come to thee, taking the oath of allegiance *at thy hands* that they will not associate anything with Allah, and that they will not steal, and will not commit adultery, nor kill their children, nor bring forth a scandalous charge which they themselves have deliberately forged, nor disobey thee in what is right, then accept their allegiance and ask Allah to forgive them. Verily, Allah is Most Forgiving, Merciful.

91. Al-Mumtaḥinah, 60:13

This verse emphasizes that the pledge of *bai'at* should be taken from women so that they will not perform *shirk*, nor steal, nor commit adultery, nor kill their children (i.e. they will be mindful of proper upbringing of their children), nor accuse anyone falsely, and nor disobey in anything good. Here, the question arises whether a Prophet, who is appointed by Allah, can ever give a command that is not good. If a Prophet can do so, then can a *Khalīfah* also give commands that are not good? In this regard, it must be clearly understood that a Prophet can never give any such command. A Prophet will only say what is right; he will not say anything otherwise. That is why at many places in the Holy Qur'ān it is mentioned that one must obey the commands of Allah and His Prophet, and one must carry them out. Nowhere is it specified that you are to obey only the good commands. The question then arises, why are there two different instructions? As a matter of fact, these are not differing instructions. Some people have made an error in understanding them. So, as I said earlier, all commandments coming from a Prophet are good. A Prophet can never give a command that is against the command of Allah or the commands of the *sharī'ah*. He is appointed by Allah to carry out those commands so how can he go against them? It is good news for you that by accepting the Prophet—the one commissioned by God—and by entering into his fold, you have become secure because no command given to you is wrong. Every command given to you is favoured by Allah.

Definition of '*Ma'rūf*' and '*Ghair Ma'rūf*'

Sometimes people move away from the organisation, mislead others, and create problems in their circle by getting caught the tangle of obedience only in '*mar'ūf*' decisions and good commands. They should understand not to delve into the definition of '*mar'ūf*' and '*ghair mar'ūf*' decisions on their own accord. Ḥaḍrat Khalīfatul Masīḥ I[ra] explaining this states:

> There is one more error and that is in understanding of the 'obedience in good things' that we will not obey in those matters that we think are not 'good'. This word has also come with reference to the Holy Prophet[sa].[92]
>
> وَلَا يَعْصِينَكَ فِي مَعْرُوفٍ
>
> Have these people made a list of faults of the Holy Prophet[sa] also? Similarly, Ḥaḍrat Ṣāḥib has written 'obedience in good things' in his conditions of *bai'at*. There is wisdom in it. I do not doubt anyone of you at all. I have explained these things lest anyone of you be deceived subtly. (*Khuṭabāt-e-Nūr*, *p.* 420–421)

The Promised Messiah[as] expounding on the subject of 'enjoins them to do good' writes:

> This Prophet directs you in matters that are not opposed to sane reason. And he prohibits you from things that common sense also prohibits you from. And he makes pure things lawful and impure things unlawful. And he removes the burdens from the nations that they were buried under. And he

92. Al-Mumtaḥinah, 60:13

> frees them from shackles that were preventing their necks from being straightened. Therefore, these people who will believe in him and will strengthen him by joining him and will help him and will follow the light that has been brought down with him, they will escape the hardships of this world and the hereafter. (*Barāhīn-e-Aḥmadiyyah*, vol. 5, *Rūḥānī Khazā'in*, vol. 21, p. 420)

Thus, just as a Prophet does not deviate from the commandments of Allah the Almighty, his *Khalīfah*—who is appointed by Allah the Almighty through a party of believers—also perpetuates the same teaching, the same commandments that Allah the Almighty has conveyed to us through the Holy Prophet[sa]. In this age, they have been explained to us by the Promised Messiah[as] in accordance with the prophecies of the Holy Prophet[sa]. So now, this system of *khilāfat* has been established in the Jamā'at through the Promised Messiah[as] in accordance with the prophecies of the Holy Prophet[sa], and it will last, *inshā' Allah*, till the end of time. Through it, decisions have been made according to *sharī'ah* and wisdom and will continue to be this way, *inshā' Allah*. These are the 'good decisions'. If, at any time, the *Khalīfah* of the time makes such a decision because of a mistake or misunderstanding, that carries the risk of causing some harm, then Allah the Almighty will bring about such means that will prevent bad consequences. In this regard, Ḥaḍrat Muṣleḥ-e-Mau'ūd[ra] states:

> It is possible that the *Khalīfah* of the time makes a mistake in personal matters. But in such matters on which depends the physical and spiritual progress, even if he commits an error,

> Allah the Almighty safeguards His Jamā'at and somehow makes him aware of the error. In the terminology of sages, it is called 'lesser sanctity'. That means, the Prophets enjoy a 'greater sanctity' but the *khulafā'* have 'lesser sanctity' and Allah the Almighty does not permit any such major mistakes by them that may cause disaster for the Jamā'at. Their decisions may have partial and minor mistakes, but in the end, the result will be victory for Islām and defeat for its enemies. Thus, because the *khulafā'* enjoy 'lesser sanctity', their policy will emanate from Allah's. While it is true that they will be the one speaking, their tongues will be in motion, their hands will move, their minds will work, yet behind all of this will be the hand of Allah. They can make minor errors in finer details. Sometimes their advisors can give them wrong advice. But crossing these intermediary obstacles, they will be the one who will be victorious. And when all the links are put together, the resulting chain will be good and it will be so strong that no power will be able to break it. (*Tafsīr-e-Kabīr,* Ḥaḍrat Mirzā Bashīr-ud-Dīn Maḥmūd Aḥmad[ra], vol. 6, p. 376–377)

From this, it is evident that 'not good' is that which is a blatant violation of commandments of Allah the Almighty and the instructions of the *sharī'ah*. Ḥaḍrat 'Alī[ra] narrates that the Holy Prophet[sa] sent away an expedition and appointed a leader for it so people should listen to him and obey him. He had a fire set up and commanded his companions to jump into it. Some people did not obey him and said, 'We have become Muslims to escape the fire.' But some people were prepared to jump into the fire. When the Holy Prophet[sa] heard of this, he observed that, 'If they had jumped into the fire, they would have stayed in it forever.' He also said, 'No obedience is obligatory if it involves disobedience to Allah. Obedience is necessary only in 'good decisions'. (*Sunano Abī Dāwūd*, Kitāb-ul-Jihād)

Further explanation of this *ḥadīth* is found in the narration of Ḥaḍrat Abū Sa'īd Khudrī[ra] who narrates that:

> The Holy Prophet[sa] sent Ḥaḍrat 'Alqamah Bin Mujazziz[ra] on a battle. When he reached there or was on the way, a contingent of his army asked for permission to proceed separately. He gave them permission and appointed Ḥaḍrat 'Abdullāh Bin Ḥudhāfah[ra] Bin Qais al-Sahmī as their leader. I was among those who went with him. While they were in journey, they set up fire for keeping warm or for cooking. 'Abdullāh Bin Ḥudhāfah[ra] (who had a humorous nature) said, 'Is it not obligatory on you to obey what I say?' They said, 'Why not?' Upon this 'Abdullāh Bin Ḥudhāfah[ra] said, 'Will you obey any command I give you?' They said, 'Yes we will obey it.' 'Abdullāh Bin Ḥudhāfah[ra] said, 'I do tell you to jump into this fire.' On this, some people stood up and started preparing to jump into the fire. When 'Abdullāh Bin Ḥudhāfah[ra] saw that they were actually going to jump into the fire, he asked them to stop themselves from doing so. Upon our return, the Companions reported it to the Holy Prophet[sa]. The Holy Prophet[sa] said, 'If any one of your leaders tells you to disobey Allah the Almighty, you should not obey him.' (*Sunano Ibn-e-Mājah*, Kitāb-ul-Jihād, Bābu Lā Ṭā'ata fī Ma'ṣiyatillāh)

One thing is quite evident from this *ḥadīth*—the decision not to obey was not of one individual. Some people were prepared to jump into the fire on account of the order to obey their leader under all circumstances. They had heard and thought that it was the Islāmic teaching to obey the leader in every way, in every condition, and in every form. But some Companions[ra] who had better understanding of the commandments of Allah, and had benefited more from the company of the Holy Prophet[sa], refused. They did not act upon it because it was suicidal, and suicide is expressly prohibited in Islām. Secondly, when 'Abdullāh Bin Ḥudhāfah[ra], who was their leader, saw the seriousness of a few, he too grew worried and stopped them because it was only a joke. After this, the Holy Prophet[sa], by his explanation, defined the principle of 'goodness' as to what is 'good' and what is 'not good'. It should be clear that a Prophet or the *Khalīfah* of the time can never say such a thing even as a joke. That is why Allah the Almighty has said that if you see a violation of a clear command by a leader, you should have recourse to Allah and the Prophet. Now in this age, righteous *khilāfat* has been established after the Promised Messiah[as]. You should turn to the *Khalīfah*. His decision will always be the 'good decision'. His decision will be in accordance with the commandment of Allah and the Prophet[sa]. Therefore, as I said earlier, you have the good news that now you are always under 'good decisions'.

These days, one might hear criticism that a worker who was doing a good job was replaced, and therefore the *Khalīfah* of the time or the organisation of the Jamā'at had not made a 'good decision'. (Such critics have made their own definition of good decisions). Therefore, they think that they have the right to speak against the decision wherever and whenever. First of all, no one has the right to speak against the Jamā'at anywhere. I have already explained this topic in depth. Your duty is only to obey. What is the standard of obedience? Allah the Almighty says in the Holy Qur'ān:[93]

وَاَقْسَمُوْا بِاللّٰهِ جَهْدَ اَيْمَانِهِمْ لَئِنْ اَمَرْتَهُمْ لَيَخْرُجُنَّ. قُلْ لَا تُقْسِمُوْا. طَاعَةٌ مَّعْرُوْفَةٌ. اِنَّ اللّٰهَ خَبِيْرٌ بِمَا تَعْمَلُوْنَ

> And they swear by Allah their strongest oaths that, if thou command them, they will surely go forth. Say, 'Swear not; *what is required is actual* obedience in what is right. Surely, Allah is well aware of what you do.'

The subject of obedience is being discussed in the preceding verses. Believers always say that we heard and accepted. Because of their piety, they are granted nearness [to Allah] and become triumphant. In this verse, we are enjoined to adopt the 'hear and obey' attitude like true believers. Do not swear that we will do this and that. Ḥaḍrat Muṣleḥ-e-Mau'ūd[ra] has written in its commentary that the hypocrites also make a lot of claims. But the good way is to practice obedience. Allah the Almighty is commanding that such people should adopt the good way to practice obedience according to the proper standard. Be obedient according to the proper customs. The Prophet is not going to give you a command that is against the *sharī'ah* and against common sense. For example, the Promised Messiah[as] says that when you have accepted me, you

93. Al Nūr, 24:54

should get used to five daily Prayers, give up falsehood, give up arrogance, stop usurping the rights of others, and live together in love and affection. All this comes under the command of 'obey in all good matters'. There are people that do not follow any of this, but instead go around saying that they swear they would do whatever is commanded to them. Similarly, there are different initiatives from *khulafā'* at different times for the spiritual growth such as about populating the mosques, proper upbringing of children, having more tolerance, courage, and calling people towards Allah, or about different financial sacrifices. These are the matters that one need to obey. In other words, these come under the classification of obedience in 'good matters'. A Prophet or a *Khalīfah* is not going to ask anything that is against the Divine commandments or common sense; he is not going to command one to jump into fire or plunge into an ocean. Prophets or *khulafā'* are always going to lead one along the *sharī'ah*.

Superior Example of Obedience

We find a great example of obedience with the Muslims of the early era when Ḥaḍrat 'Umar[ra] took the command away from Ḥaḍrat Khālid[ra] Bin al-Walīd and gave it to Ḥaḍrat Abū 'Ubaidah[ra] in the course of a battle. Thinking that Khālid[ra] Bin al-Walīd was performing well, Ḥaḍrat Abū 'Ubaidah[ra] did not take over the charge from him right away. When Ḥaḍrat Khālid[ra] Bin al-Walīd learnt that this command had come from Ḥaḍrat 'Umar[ra], he went to Ḥaḍrat Abū 'Ubaidah[ra] and said, 'Since it is the instruction from the *Khalīfah* of the time, you should implement it without any delay. I have no reservation in serving under your command, and I will continue to work as hard under you as I did when I was the commander.' This is the high standard of obedience. Some foolish person can say that it was 'not a good decision' of Ḥaḍrat 'Umar[ra]. This is also a wrong notion. We do not know the circumstances as to why Ḥaḍrat 'Umar[ra] made that decision. He knew it better. There was nothing obvious in this decision that would be against the *sharī'ah*. Note that Allah the Almighty upheld the honour of this decision of Ḥaḍrat 'Umar[ra] and the battle was won. During the battle, some occasions were such that there were a hundred enemy soldiers against a single Muslim soldier, yet the battle was won.

The Promised Messiah[as] also received the distinction to be an arbitrator and a judge in the service of his Master—a service that is unparalleled. Therefore, in this age, the claim of obedience and love for the Holy Prophet[sa] and the claim for love for Allah can be justified by true obedience to the Promised Messiah[as], just as Allah the Almighty says:[94]

قُلْ اِنْ كُنْتُمْ تُحِبُّوْنَ اللّٰهَ فَاتَّبِعُوْنِىْ يُحْبِبْكُمُ اللّٰهُ وَيَغْفِرْلَكُمْ ذُنُوْبَكُمْ ۔
وَاللّٰهُ غَفُوْرٌ رَّحِيْمٌ

Say, 'If you love Allah, follow me: *then* will Allah love you and forgive you your faults. And Allah is most Forgiving, Merciful.'

94. Āl-e-'Imrān, 3:32

Whatever Promised Messiah[as] Attained was by Following the Holy Prophet Muḥammad[sa]

The Promised Messiah[as] states:

> I have received a full measure of the blessing that were given to the Prophets and honoured ones of God before me purely as a result of the Grace of Allah and not due to any merit of my own. And it was not possible for me to get this blessing if I did not follow the ways of my Master and Lord, the honour of the Prophets and the best of them all, the Holy Prophet[sa]. So, whatever I achieved, resulted from following the path of the Holy Prophet[sa]. I understand—based on my true and complete knowledge—that no one can reach God without following His Prophet[sa], nor can he have a share of the perfect understanding. And here I am going to tell you about the first thing that develops in the heart as a result of the honest and perfect following of the Holy Prophet[sa]; so know it that it is the righteous heart. The love of the world departs from the heart, and it desires an eternal and unending pleasure. Then, as a consequence of this righteous heart, a pure and perfect Divine love is acquired. And all these blessings are received as inheritance from following the Holy Prophet[sa]. As Allah the Almighty Himself states:[95]
>
> قُلْ اِنْ كُنْتُمْ تُحِبُّوْنَ اللّٰهَ فَاتَّبِعُوْنِىْ يُحْبِبْكُمُ اللّٰهُ

95. Āl-e-'Imrān, 3:32

That is:

Tell them if you love God, come follow me so that God may love you too.

Indeed, a one-sided claim of love is totally false and absurd. When man honestly loves God, then God also loves him. Then an acceptance for him is spread in the world. A sincere love for him is produced in the hearts of thousands; a force of attraction is granted to him, and a light is given to him that always stays with him. When a person loves Allah with a sincere heart and adopts Him over the whole world and to him nothing is left of the majesty and dignity of anything besides Allah—instead he considers all these others to be worse than a dead worm—then Allah Who sees his heart descends upon it with a weighty manifestation. Just as a refined mirror put in front of the sun provides a so perfect reflection of the sun that it can be said, figuratively and metaphorically, that the same sun that is in the sky is also present in the mirror, likewise Allah descends on such a heart and makes it His throne. This is the purpose for which man was created. (*Ḥaqīqat-ul-Waḥyi, Rūḥānī Khazā'in*, vol. 22, p. 64–65)

As a result of the love and the affection the Promised Messiah[as] had for the Holy Prophet[sa], Allah the Almighty made the heart of the Promised Messiah[as] a part of His throne. Allah will continue to descend upon the hearts in the future also according to their respective statures. But now the claim of the love for the Holy Prophet[sa], the claim of his perfect obedience, will prove true only when the bond of love and obedience with his spiritual son is established. That is why the Promised Messiah[as] says, 'Establish a bond of love and obedience with me above all other relations. This is how one will follow the Holy Prophet[sa] and subsequently attain Allah's love.' He is not saying this lightly. The Holy Prophet[sa] himself has told us this as he said, 'If you see the time of Messiah and Mahdī, you should go and convey my *salām* to him even if you have to crawl on your knees.' What is the message in this emphasis in taking so much pain to convey this *salām*? What is the wisdom behind it? The Holy Prophet[sa] is pointing out that the Promised Messiah is dear to him and he is dear to the Promised Messiah. This is matter of principle that you reach the ones you love through their loved ones. Therefore, he says, 'If you want to become my follower, follow the Promised Messiah, accept him as the *Imām*, and enter his Jamā'at.' That is why it is said in a *ḥadīth*:

> 'Beware! There will be no Prophet or Messenger between Jesus the son of Mary (the Promised Messiah) and me. Listen carefully that he will be my *Khalīfah* from among my followers after me. He will certainly kill *Dajjāl*, he will shatter the cross, meaning he will destroy the Christian doctrine, and he will abolish *jizyah* [poll tax]. (In the period of the Promised Messiah[as], its practice will be abandoned because there will be no religious wars.) Remember, anyone who gets the honour of meeting him, he must convey my *salām* to him. (*Al-Mo'jam Al-ausaṭ waṣ-Ṣaghīr Liṭ-ṭabarānī*)

Instead of reflecting on this *ḥadīth* and instead of listening to those who have reflected on it and have unlocked its depth, the scholars of this day have gone after its literal meaning and have misled simple-minded Muslims and have created such a havoc that is beyond belief. We seek the protection of Allah from them, and He is dealing with them and will deal with them in the future, *inshā' Allah*. It is evident from this *ḥadīth* that the Promised Messiah[as] will be a just ruler; he will not do anything against justice, and he is such an *Imām* who will establish equity in the world. Therefore, establish contact with him, follow his commands, and act on his teachings because he will only teach justice and equity, and this is nothing but Qur'ānic teachings. People of this age expect that the Messiah will come with hammers and will literally shatter the cross. This is absurdity. It is quite obvious that the Promised Messiah, following his master and patron, will convince others through arguments, and through arguments he will annihilate and expose the Christian doctrine. What is meant by the killing of the *Dajjāl* is only that the Promised Messiah will save the *ummah* from the mischief of the *Dajjāl*. Moreover, since there will be no religious wars, the practice of a poll tax will also cease. Then, there is the instruction to convey the *salām* to the Promised Messiah, but the Muslims, instead of conveying the *salām*, are bent upon opposing the Promised Messiah[as]. May Allah grant them sense.

There is another tradition from which we learn the status of the Promised Messiah[as] and the reason it is essential for us to maintain a bond of obedience with him.

> Ḥaḍrat Abū Hurairah[ra] narrates that the Holy Prophet[sa] said, 'Until Jesus, son of Mary, who is a Just Ruler and Equitable *Imām*, appears, the end of days will not come. [When he is sent], he will break the cross, kill the swine, abolish *jizyah* and will distribute such treasures that people will not be ready to accept.' (*Sunano Ibn-e-Mājah*, Kitābul-Fitan, Bābu Fitnatid-

Dajjāli wa Khurūji 'Īsabni Maryama wa Khurūji Yājūja wa Mājūj)

Since this *ḥadīth* also required interpretation, it was not understood by the people of coarse intellect and they went after its literal meaning giving it an odd and ridiculous explanation. It is quite obvious that 'killing the swine' pertains to eliminating those people with swine-like characters. The faults of swine compared to other animals are now well-known. When the same faults appear in humans, obviously their cleansing is very much needed. Another point not understood by such [people of coarse intellect] is that he will give and distribute wealth. Just a few days ago, some 'scholars' held a gathering in Pakistan, and using extremely vulgar language against the Promised Messiah[as] and the Jamā'at, they raised this question that the Messiah was to come and distribute wealth and not to ask people for it. Yet, Aḥmadīs (they instead say Qādiānīs) collect *chandah* [donations], which proves that they are imposters. No sane person can make them understand that these are the spiritual treasures that the Messiah[as] is distributing that they refuse to accept. The fact of the matter is that they only have the eye for this world and they cannot go beyond it. This is their role. Let them continue. Pakistani Aḥmadīs need not be too apprehensive. In the face of these scholars' filth and absurdities, we should walk away displaying patience and fortitude. In the face of these scholars' filth and absurdities, we do admit that we accept our defeat; we cannot compete with their filth and absurdities. I must make one point very clear that when man does not say anything, Allah speaks for him, and when Allah speaks, we have seen the pieces of the enemy scattered all over, and we shall see that in the future also, *inshā' Allah*. Therefore, Aḥmadīs should have a loyal relationship with the Promised Messiah[as] and place emphasis upon prayers. Continue to pray all the time.

These traditions also prove that the Messiah to come will also be the *Imām*. He will also be the *Ḥakam* [Authority]. He will be the prince of justice and equity. You must establish a bond with him, and it is incumbent on you to obey him as the *Ḥakam* and the *Imām*. These teachings are for your betterment and training. You should act upon them so that you join those who are dear to the Holy Prophet[sa] and who have achieved nearness to Allah the Almighty.

Submission Under All Circumstances

I shall present some traditions that illustrate the importance of submission.

> Ḥaḍrat Abū Hurairah[ra] states that the Holy Prophet[sa] said, 'It is incumbent on you to listen to and obey the directives of the ruler of the time in austerity or prosperity, happiness or grief, inequity or favouritism—in any and all situations.' (*Ṣaḥīḥ Muslim*, Kitāb-ul-Imārah)

> Ḥaḍrat Ibn-e-'Abbās[ra] states that the Prophet of Allah said, 'If anyone sees something undesirable in his leader and ruler, he should exercise patience because, if anyone is even slightly distant from the Jamā'at, he will die in ignorance.' (*Ṣaḥīḥ Al-Bukhārī*, Kitābul- Fitan, Bābu Qaulin-Nabiyyi Sa-tarauna Ba'dī Umūran)

Ḥaḍrat 'Arfajah[ra] states that, 'I heard the Holy Prophet[sa] saying that when you are gathered together on one hand and have one leader, if someone comes and tries to break your unity so that he may create divisions among you, you ought to kill him. That is, you should cut your ties with him and not listen to him, (i.e., totally ignore his instructions). (*Ṣaḥīḥ Muslim,* Kitāb-ul-Imārah, Bābu Ḥukmi man Farraqa Amral-Muslimīna wa huwa Mujtami'un)

It is reported from Ḥaḍrat 'Ubādah[ra] Bin Aṣ-Sāmit[ra] that we took the covenant with the Holy Prophet[sa] on the point that we will listen and we will obey whether we like it or dislike it. And that wherever we are, we will not dispute with the incumbant of rightful authority, we will stay firm on the truth or that we will only speak the truth and that we will not be afraid of the rebuke of anyone in matters concerning Allah the Almighty. (*Ṣaḥīḥ Muslim,* Kitāb-ul-Imārah, Bābu wujūdi Ṭā'atil-Umarā'i)

Ḥaḍrat Ibn-e-'Umar[ra] states that the Holy Prophet[sa] said, 'Whoever holds back from obedience to Allah will meet Allah the Almighty on the Day of Judgement in a condition that he would have no valid argument or excuse. And he who dies in a condition that he has not taken a pledge of allegiance with the *Imām* of the time would die the death of ignorance and apostasy.' (*Ṣaḥīḥ Muslim,* Kitāb-ul-Imārah, Bāb-ul-Amri bi Luzūmil-Jamā'ati 'Inda Ẓuhūril-Fitan)

Thus, you are fortunate that you have accepted the *Imām* of the time and you have entered into a covenant of *bai'at* with him. Now, you have to obey him purely for the sake of Allah.

You have to carry out all his commandments. Otherwise, you will be going out of the circle of obedience to Allah the Almighty. May Allah establish every Aḥmadī on the superior standard of obedience. And how do you establish such high standards? These standards can be achieved only by acting on the teachings of the Promised Messiah[as].

Who Enters the Jamā'at

The Promised Messiah[as] says:

> Only he enters my Jamā'at who adopts my teachings as the code of his life and acts upon them according to his capacity and capability. But the one who just gets his name registered but does not act according to the teachings should be mindful that Allah has decreed to make this Jamā'at a special Jamā'at, and anyone who does not truly belong to this Jamā'at will not be counted among it just because he has registered. A time will come upon him that he would dissociate himself. Therefore, as far as possible, make your deeds subservient to the teaching that is given.

What is that teaching? He says:

> Do not say anything that will create disorder, do no evil, show patience in the face of abuse, and do not confront anyone. If someone confronts you, treat him kindly and gently. Set a good example of soft speech. Honestly obey every command so that God may be pleased with you, and the enemy should realise that after taking the covenant, you are no longer the same person that you were. Testify honestly in litigation.

> Everyone who enters this Jamā'at should adopt righteousness with all his heart, determination, and strength. The world is nearing its end. (*Malfūẓāt*, new ed., vol. 3, p. 620–621)

Here, he has said that you should not say anything that will create disorder. Some people are in the habit of spreading rumours for fun. That carries the risk of creating disorder. People have different temperaments. If something unpleasant is stated in the presence of the one who was the subject of that comment, that person will naturally develop a resentment against the person to whom the statement is attributed. Though I feel that it should not produce any ill feeling, there is a way to stop such mischief, and that is that one should directly approach the person to whom the comment was attributed and ask him, 'Have you heard these comments; have you said anything like this?' That will clarify the matter and will also help reform the mischief-makers. Sometimes such mischief-makers pit families against families. Stay away from such mischief and from such mischief-makers. And if possible, try to reform such people.

Evil also develops from direct confrontations, fights and abuses. That also creates discord. The Promised Messiah[as] tells us: if you are connected to me and you claim submission to me, then shun everything of mischief and evil. You should have such patience and tolerance that even if someone abuses you, you should show restraint. The door of salvation will open for you when you act upon this teaching. You will join those who have achieved nearness to Allah. There should be no confrontation in any matter. Even being in the right, be humble like one who is in the wrong. No matter what the other person has said, deal with that person with love, affection and sincerity. Your tongue should be so pure, your language so sweet, and good morals so overflowing that people should be attracted towards you. Everyone should realise that you are an Aḥmadī. Nothing less than the highest moral values can be expected of you. In short, your high morals will attract others and will become a source for drawing their attention.

Some people give false testaments for personal gain in litigation. They present their case falsely. The Promised Messiah[as] says that even your vested interests should not prevent you from truthful testimony. Some people here and in other countries make false statements in their efforts to migrate. Stay away from all these things. Submit your [migration] case based on the facts, and if it is granted as such, then you should stay; otherwise you should go back. Sometimes cases are rejected even if they are fabricated; you should try sticking to the truth. *Inshā' Allah*, it will only benefit you. Even if your case is rejected, you will at least not earn the displeasure of Allah.

Develop Brotherhood and Love Among Yourselves and a True Relationship With Allah the Almighty

Advising about mutual love and brotherhood, the Promised Messiah[as] says:

> Develop brotherhood and love among yourselves and give up viciousness and dissension. Totally abstain from any kind of insult and ridicule because they distance you from truth and

lead you far away. Treat each other with respect. Everyone should give priority to the comfort of his brother. Create a sincere reconciliation with Allah the Almighty and come back into His obedience.... Get rid of every kind of dispute, hostility and animosity from among yourselves because the time has come that we should abstain from petty matters and become preoccupied with important and magnificent goals. (*Malfūẓāt*, vol. 1. p. 268–288)

Then he says:

> Our Jamā'at should have a sincere relationship with Allah the Almighty, and the Jamā'at members should be grateful that Allah has not rejected them. Instead, he has shown hundreds of signs of His power to elevate their faith to the level of conviction. Is there anyone among you who can say that he has not seen any sign? I do claim that there is not even one who has had the occasion to stay in my company and yet not seen a fresh sign from Allah with his own eyes.
>
> This is what our Jamā'at needs—that their faith be enhanced, that they should develop true conviction and understanding of Allah, that there should be no laziness or indifference about the righteous deeds. If one is lazy, and it is a hardship even to perform ablution, how would he offer *tahajjud* [supererogatory Prayers]. If the strength to perform the righteous deeds and the passion to excel in goodness do not develop, it is useless to establish a link with us. (*Malfūẓāt*, new ed., vol. 2. p. 710–711)

In this tenth condition of *bai'at*, the Promised Messiah[as] has placed great emphasis on having such a strong bond with him that there should be nothing like it in any other relationship of this world. The only reason for this emphasis is, strictly speaking, his sympathy for us. Because the true Islām can be found only and only by accepting him, if we want to save ourselves from drowning, then we have to get on the ark of the Promised Messiah[as].

He says:

> Now rush towards me because this is the time that he who runs toward me now is like the one who gets on board the ship right at the time of a storm. But if someone does not accept me, I see that he is throwing himself into a storm and has no means of saving himself. I am a true intercessor as a shadow and reflection of that Exalted intercessor, who was not accepted by the ignorant people of that age and who was gravely insulted, that is Ḥaḍrat Muḥammad the Chosen one, may peace and blessings of Allah be upon him. (*Dāfi'ul-Balā'*. *Rūḥānī Khazā'in*, vol. 18 p. 223)

He said this because the claim of the Promised Messiah[as] is in accordance with the prophecies of the Holy Prophet[sa].

Two Benefits of Bai'at at the Hand of Promised Messiah[as]

Then he says:

> Thus, there are two benefits of this *bai'at* that is done at my hand. One is that the sins are forgiven and one is entitled to clemency in accordance with the promise of Allah the Almighty. The other is that by repenting in the presence of the

Apostle, strength is granted and man is saved from the attacks of Satan. Be mindful that the world should not be your objective when you enter this Movement, but your objective should be the pleasure of Allah, because this world is only a passing phase and will pass by one way or the other.[96]

؎ شب تنور گذشت و شب سمور گذشت۔

Keep this world and its objectives and purposes entirely aside. Do not mix them with faith because this world is doomed to end, but the faith and its rewards are unending. (*Malfūẓāt*, vol. 6, p. 145)

The Promised Messiah[as]—the Strong Fort of Protection for Our Times

The Promised Messiah[as] says:

O ye dear ones, O ye the flourishing branches of the tree of my being, who, by the mercy of God Almighty, which you enjoy because of having entered into the covenant of *bai'at* with me! you are devoting your lives, comfort, and properties to this cause. I am aware that you will deem it your good fortune to carry out whatever I might impose upon you to the full extent of your capacity. But I do not desire to lay down anything by myself as an obligation upon you, so that your service should not be the result of my directive, but should proceed out of your own free will. Who is my friend and who is dear to me? Only he who recognises me. Only he who believes that I have been sent and accepts me as those are

96. *A night of pleasure or a night of sorrow; the night will pass either way.*

accepted who are sent. The world cannot accept me because I am not of the world, but those whose natures have been invested with a portion of the other world accept me and will accept me. He who turns away from me, turns aside from Him Who has sent me. And he who establishes a relationship with me establishes a relationship with Him from Whom I have come. I hold a lamp in my hand. He who comes to me will surely partake of its light, but he who, out of ill-thinking, runs away will be cast into the darkness. I am the citadel of security for this age. He who enters therein will be secure against thieves and robbers and wild beasts. He who seeks to remain away from my walls will be confronted with death from every direction, and even his dead body will not be saved. Who is it who enters my citadel? Only he who discards vice and adopts goodness, and gives up crookedness and treads along the path of truth, and frees himself from the bondage of Satan and becomes an obedient servant of Allah the Almighty. Everyone who does that is in me, and I am in him. But only he has the power to attain to this upon whom Allah the Almighty bestows a pure soul. Then He places His foot in the hell of such a one's inner self, and it becomes cool as if there had never been any fire in it. Then he marches forward till the spirit of Allah the Almighty dwells in him, and, with a special manifestation, the Lord of the world establishes Himself in his heart. Then his old humanity is consumed and a new and pure humanity is bestowed on him. For him Allah the Almighty becomes a new Allah and establishes a special relationship with him and he is equipped in this very life with the pure fittings of a heavenly life. (*Fat-ḥe-Islām*, *Rūḥānī Khazā'in*, vol. 3, p. 34–35)

May Allah the Almighty enable us all to fulfil all our pledges made with the Promised Messiah[as]; may we remain firmly established upon all the conditions of his *bai'at*; may we, by acting upon his teachings, make our lives like paradise, and may we be judged to be the inheritors of the paradises of the next world. May Allah the Almighty help us. *Āmīn*.

INDEX OF NAMES

Abraham 59, 139, 142
Abū ʻUbaidah 177
Abū ʻUbaidah Bin Jarrāḥ........ 141
Abū Burdah Bin Abī Muṣā 63
Abū Hurairah ..22, 32, 35, 38, 51, 56–57, 68, 79, 91, 124–125, 133–135, 152, 154, 156, 182, 184
Abū Muṣā al-Ashʻarī 109
Abū Raihanah 27
Abū Saʻid Khudrī........... 28, 125, 133–134
Abū Shuraiḥ 27
Abū Ṭalḥah Anṣārī................ 141
Abū Dhar al-Ghaffārī.............. 82
Adam....................................... 66
Anas Bin Mālīk............. 115, 141
Asmā' Bint Yazīd.................... 40
Aswad..................................... 32
ʻAbdul Karīm........................ 162
ʻAbdullāh Bin ʻAmr Bin al-ʻĀṣ..... .... 21–22, 59
ʻAbdullāh Bin Ḥudhāfah 174
ʻAlī 153
ʻIyāḍullāh Bin ʻAbdullāh 3
ʻUbadah Bin As-Ṣāmit 3, 4, 28, 114, 185
ʻUrwah Bin Muḥammad.......... 83
ʻAbdul Wahhāb Bin al-Ward ... 95
ʻAbdullāh 126
ʻAbdullāh Bin ʻUmar...... 154, 156
ʻAbdullāh Bin Ḥudhāfah Bin Qais al-Sahmi.................... 174–175
ʻAbdullāh bin Masʻūd.. 21, 34, 60, 124,153
ʻAbdullāh Ibn-e-Masʻūd... 22, 153
ʻAbdur-Raḥmān Bin ʻAmr As-Salamī.......................... 114
ʻAbdur Raḥmān Bin Shibl........32
ʻAishah...............4–5, 94–95, 104
ʻAlqamah Bin Mujazziz 174
ʻAmīr Bin Rabīʻah 60
ʻAmr Bin al-ʻAuf................... 105
ʻArfajah 185
ʻIrbāḍ Bin Sāriyah 114
ʻIyāḍ Bin Ḥimār al-Mujāshiʻī . 133
ʻUmar 177–178
ʻUmar Bin al-Khaṭṭāb..............60
ʻUtbah 83
Bilāl 56
Fāṭimah.................................. 135
Ḥujr Bin Ḥujr........................ 114
Ibn-e-ʻAbbās............. 63, 93, 184
Ibn-e-ʻUmar 185
Ibn-e-Masʻūd 22, 123
Imām Ḥusain 76–77
Imām Mālik 21
Jaʻfar Bin Abī Ṭālib 135

Jābir.............................. 104, 123
Khālid Bin al-Walīd 177
Luqmān 14, 122
Maulānā Nūr-ud-Dīn 9
Mu'ādh............................. 68–69
Mu'ādh Bin Jabal.................... 40
Mu'āwiyah............................. 95
Mu'āwiyah Bin Ḥaidah
al-Qushairī........................ 140
Muḥammad Bin Ibrāhīm 94
Muḥammad Bin Sīrīn 26
Munshī 'Abdullāh[ra] of Sanour.... 9
No'mān Bin Bashīr 68
Ṣāḥibzādah Sayyed 'Abdul Laṭīf
Shahīd..................................98
Sheikh 'Abdur-Raḥmān Khān
....98
Ṣūfī Aḥmad Jān 7, 9
Sufyān...................................140
Ṣuhaib Bin Sinān......................91
Ubayy Bin Ka'ab....................141
Usaid 92
Yūsuf......................................45
Ziyād 83

VERSES OF THE HOLY QUR'ĀN

Chapter Index

Chapter	Verse	Page
Āl-e-'Imrān	3:133	113
Āl-e-'Imrān	3:135	76–78
Āl-e-'Imrān	3:32	115–116, 178–179
Al-Nisā'	4:37	147, 159
Al-'Aṣr	103:4	25
Al-A'rāf	7:24	66
Al-Aḥzāb	33:36	25
Al-Aḥzāb	33:57	58
Al-An'ām	6:153	24
Al-Anfāl	8:2	113
Al-Anfāl	8:34	63
Al-Baqarah	2:113	138–139
Al-Baqarah	2:194	41
Al-Baqarah	2:208	89
Al-Baqarah	2:218	42
Al-Baqarah	2:283–284	24
Al-Bayyinah	98:6	137–138
Al-Dahr	76:11	159
Al-Dahr	76:12	160
Al-Dahr	76:9	86, 149–151
Al-Fajr	89:28–31	90–91
Al-Fātiḥah	1:2	67–68
Al-Furqān	25:64	132
Al-Furqān	25:73	25
Al-Ḥajj	22:31	20, 23–24
Al-Ḥujurāt	49:8	31–32

Chapter	Verse	Page
Al-Mā'idah	5:36	61
Al-Mā'idah	5:9	24
Al-Mu'minūn	23:6	44
Al-Mumtaḥinah	60:13	4, 169, 171
Al-Najm	53:38	142
Al-Naṣr	110:4	63
Al-Nāzi'āt	79:41–42	104
Al-Nāzi'āt	79:41	107
Al-Nisā'	4:108	38
Al-Nisā'	4:49	13
Al-Nisā'	4:126	139
Al-Nisā'	4:136	24
Al-Nisā'	4:60	112–113
Al-Nūḥ	11:13	62
Al-Nūr	24:31	29
Al-Nūr	24:54	176
Al-Nūr	24:57	50
Al-Qamar	54:18	109
Al-Qaṣaṣ	28:51	103
Al-Qaṣaṣ	28:78	39
Al-Shur'āra'	26:41	77
Al-Zukhruf	43:66	34
Al-Zumar	39:4	20, 46
Al-Zumar	39:54	62
Banī Isrā'īl	17:33	26
Banī Isrā'īl	17:38	121
Banī Isrā'īl	17:80	55–56
Hūd	11:4	66
Hūd	11:44	45
Luqmān	31:14	14
Luqmān	31:19	122
Saba'	34:2	68
Ṭā Hā	20:15	50
Yūsuf	12:54	45

SUBJECT INDEX

A

Abraham
faithfulness of, ... 142
friendship with Allah of 139

adhān
defined xi
hearing of 59

adultery
aspects 26

Aḥmadī(s)
adopt the habit of forgivness 134
appeal to, ... 161
defined xi
fortunate to have accepted the Imām of the time 185
make obligatory to recite two to three *ruku'* of the Holy Qur'ān regularly 112
persecution of, ... 99
should avoid arrogance 125
showing patience 99
to leave the company of bad people 133
to try to be counted among the meek 135

Aḥmadiyyah Muslim Jamā'at
defined xi
history of, ... 99

'Āishah
mother of the faithful 4

alcohol
prohibition of, ... 140
wrong to befriend someone who consumes 106

Allah
accepting Messiah as a commandment of, ... 168
asking for forgiveness at the time of *bai'at* from, ... 4
associating partners with, ... 10, 14
attain the love of, ... 149
be kind to the creation of, .. 149
being true to *bai'at* will have reward with, ... 3
blessed is the one who beliefs in, ... 71
bounties on Aḥmadīs by, ... 99

by taking *bai'at*, life is sold to, ... 2
certainty in, ... 143
defined xi
develop brotherhood among yourselves and a true relationship with, ... 188
essential for all believers to believe in, ... 2
expectation from Jamā'at members by, ... 37, 41, 85
faith that lacks human sympathy is not from, ... 43
fault of His servants covered by, ... 3
grandeur, mantle of, ... 125
granting of high and low status to men by, ... 133
greater status granted by, ... 134
has the power over everything 131
helps him who is keen to help his brother 154
honour a garment of, ... 125
kind treatment to all is a commandment of, ... 148
last Jamā'at established by, ... 95
manifesting His glory through Jamā'at 8
mischievous not loved by, ... 39
one who adopt humility and humbleness, his status is raised by, ... 133
one who treats His family (creatures) well is liked by 153
praise of, ... 68
proud person disliked by, ... 123
Promised Messiah[as]
commanded the to take *bai'at* by 6
Promised Messiah[as] granted the permission to take *bai'at* by xix
Prophet can not give a command against, ... 170
remain ever-thankful to, ... 68
remain faithful to, ... 93
remembrance of, ... 40
Satan disobeyed, ... 119
secrets of the hearts known by 11
seed will grow if of a good quality by the grace of, ... 1
sincere obedience is due only to, ... 20
submission to, ... 139, 142
suffer loss due to breaking the pledge made with, ... 2
surrendering oneself to, ... 139
take *bai'at* at the conditions that one will not associate anything with, ... 3
taking a *bai'at* at the hand of Promised Messiah is taking a *bai'at* with, ... 6
unjust people not guided by, ... 103
Unity of, ... 16
taking *bai'at* that believers will not associate anything with, ... 4

taking protection besides,..... 46
teachings for acquiring the quality of chastity by,........ 30
to take *bai'at* means handing one's life to,........................ 2
treading in the path of,........... 2
wealth does not decrease when it is spent in the way of, . 134
will not forgive *shirk* 13

anger
a consequence of haughtiness and conceit.................... 136
Satan brings, ... 83
shun, ... 86

appreciation
perfect understanding root of, ... 144

arrogance
all mischief originates from, 148
as a characteristic of Satan, . 119
brings man in competition with Allah,............................ 125
dangerous disease 129
deep connection with Satan 127
due to caste or lineage........ 128
first sin that lead to eternal ruin 126
ḥadīth on staying away from, ... 123
meekness and,.................... 132
of governments................. 122
other evils breeds from,...... 123
Promised Messiah's[as] advice to Jamā'at regarding, ... 130
resulting from mental superiority...................... 130
resulting from strength 131
second only to *shirk*............ 126
what is, ... 124, 130

attractions
not to be misled by, ... 93

B

backbiting
people at their worst 40

bai'at
a source to stay away from evil of society 170
account of first, by Munshī 'Abdullāh[ra] of Sanour 9
admonishment of Promised Messiah[as] on first, ... 9
advice at the first,................... 9
aḥādīth on the subject of, ... 3–4
benefits of, at the hand of Promised Messiah[as] 190
conditions of, at the time of the Holy Prophet Muḥammad[sa] 3
defined.................................. xi
Divine commandment given to Promised Messiah[as] 6
expectations of Promised Messiah[as] from those who perform,..................... 37, 84
expected behaviour of people performing,...................... 11

first announcement regarding, 6
first, taken at the house of Ḥaḍrat Ṣūfī Aḥmad Jān 9
handing over one's life to Allah 2
fulfiling the pledge of, ... 160
giving up pride as a condition of, ... 120
Holy Prophet Muḥammad[sa] taking, from women Companions[ra] 92
linked to seed in the earth 1
meaning of, ... 1
not to forget, at the time of ease 99
of first person 9
performing *istikhārah* before taking, ... 7
Promised Messiah's[as] purpose of taking 7
purposeless to take, without sincerity 73
spending life with meekness 135
summary of ten conditions of, ... 3
to safeguard completely from carnal desires 103
what it means to join, ... 168

Bashīr I
death of, ... 6

believer(s)
guard themselves against carnal passions 44
ranks of, ... 44
recitation of Holy Qur'ān .. 109
speaks the truth 22

benevolence
showing, ... 148

blood
not needed for salvation 144

businessmen
clean dealings of, ... 33

C

caste
arrogance resulting from, ... 128

celibacy
through fasting and dieting... 30

certainty
of faith 143

Changez Khān
ruins at the hands of, ... 33

charity
wealth not reduced by giving, ... 156

chastity
Allah's teachings on five remedies 30
fasting to attain, ... 27
for those who are not able to get married 27
performing physical work to attain, ... 27

children
moral training of, ... 22
reacting to the cruelty of their fathers 122

company
influence of bad, ... 106

compassion
for Allah's creation 157
for everyone 151
for humankind 158

conceit
born out of anger 136

countries
arrogance of, ... 122

creation
kindness towards Allah's, ... 145
sympathy be shown for, ... 150

creatures
Allah's family, ... 153

cross
not needed for salvation 144

cruelty
darkness and, ... 34

customs
adopted from other religions 101
different types of frivolous,. 101
forsake frivolous, ... 103
not to follow irreligious, ... 101
refrain from unwanted, ... 108
take one away from religon 106

D

Dajjāl
creating hardship to move Aḥmadīs away from Allah and the Jamā'at 93
defined xii
killing of 182

darkness
cruelty and, ... 34

durūd
defined xii
sending upon Holy Prophet Muḥammad[sa] 58
should be recited abundantly 59

Day of Judgement
hard and long 159
person closest to Holy Prophet Muḥammad[sa] on 60, 123
person dearest to Holy Prophet Muḥammad[sa] on 123

death
funeral at the time of, ... 153
present oneself to Allah at the time of 2

deeds
questions about on Day of Judgment 135

deluge
at Noah's time 45

of carnal passions.................. 44

desires
eschew............................... 103

devotion
perfect, ... 144

dieting
as a means to attain celibacy............................... 30

disbelief
falsehood and Hell 23

discord
created by evil.................... 187
Promised Messiah's advice on avoiding,.......................... 41

dishonesty
eschew,................................ 38
ḥadīth about, ... 38

doctors
dedicated their lives for the service of humanity........ 161

domestic affairs
circle of, ... 122

E

ears
protecting from listening to prohibited voices 30

enemy
of Allah's friend 56

enmity
towards each others............. 80

essence
of the teachings of Islām..... 139

evil
adultery lies at the limit of,... 26
creates discord.................... 187
develops from direct confrontations, fights and abuses............................ 187
eschew company of,....... 38, 85
falsehood lies at the root of,..20
ḥadīth about,........................ 83
self that incites to, ... 44

eyes
lustful eye, keeping away from 27
restraining one's 30
state of purity 31

F

faith
certainty of,....................... 143
importance of,.................... 137
innovations that have nothing to do with,.................... 104
not from Allah if it lacks human sympathy.......................... 43
preference over worldly matters 137
Satan making men careless about his, ... 10

sign of true, ... 98

falsehood
adultery and, ... 26
as an idol 25
greatest of all faults 19
Hell and, ... 21–22
idolatry and, ... 23
kufr and 23
lies at the root of evil 20
natural aversion to, ... 23
shirk and, ... 20

fast(ing)
behaviour during, ... 32
breaking of, to indulge in desires 15
for appearances 128
ḥadīth about, ... 32
obligatory with certain prerequisites of, ... 53
means of attaining chastity 27, 30

father
mistreating the children 121

fear
perfect understanding is the root of, ... 144

fidelity
shown by 'Abdur-Raḥmān Khān[ra] 98
shown by Ṣāḥibzādah Sayyed 'Abdul Laṭīf Shahīd[ra] 98

fire
lying and............................ 22
people who abuse the rights of others will be in, ... 35

food
wasted, in marriage celebrations 102

forbearance
adopt, ... 77

forgiveness
adopt, ... 77
Aḥmadīs to adopt, ... 134
Allah's reward for those who practice 133
ḥadīth on, ... 134
seek, ... 86

G

ghaḍḍ-e-baṣar
defined................................ xii
what is, ... 27

ghafara
defined................................ xii
what is, ... 67

God
See Allah

good and not good
definition of, ... 171

goodness
reward of, ... 43

government(s)
arrogance of, ... 122

Islāmic, ... 43
loyalty to, ... 42

Grandeur
mantel of Allah 125

gratitude
expressing, to Allah 68

gratefulness
to Allah.......................... 43, 68

H

Ḥajj
commandment of,................ 29
defined xiii
obligatory with certain prerequisites.................... 53
performing for appearances 128

Halākū
ruin at the hands of, ... 33

ḥalāl
commandment of,................ 29
defined xiii

ḥarām
commandment of,................ 29
defined xiii

haughtiness
born out of anger.............. 136

heart
state of purity...................... 31

Heaven
be merciful on earth so that you may be shown mercy in, .. 43
filled with meek people...... 124

Hell
disbelief and, ... 23
falsehood and 21
falsehood leads to, ... 22
filled with haughty people .. 124

Hindu
sympathy for, ... 158

Holy Prophet Muḥammad[sa]
achieving grace through, ... 61
advice of, on telling the truth 19
concerned on corruption of faith 105
condition of *bai'at* at the time of, ... 3
defined................................ xiii
feared *shirk* in his *ummah* 14
humility of, ... 129
no one can reach Allah without following, ... 179
on Prayers 51
person dearest to on the Day of Judgement...................... 123
prayed fervently for the pleasure of Allah 94
raised to uproot false notions 17
status of meek in the eyes of, ... 134
subservient to the sovereignty of the, ... 103

taking pledge from women 4
taqwā in his heart.................. 78
whatever the Promised Messiah[as] attained was due to, ... 179

honesty
natural human condition...... 39

human beings
like part of body 158
nature of.............................. 23

humility
adopt, ... 86
Allah raises status of those who adopt, ... 133
ḥadīth on,.......................... 133
of Promised Messiah[as] 120

hungry
feeding of the,.................... 160

hypocrite
evil of, ... 123
four characteristics of, ... 21
recitation of Holy Qur'ān by, ... 109

I

Ibrāhīm
See Abraham

idolatry
falsehood and,............... 23, 25

types of, ... 16

Imām
defined.................................xiii
sign of true,.......................... 98

immorality
saving oneself from,.............. 31

infant
honesty and integrity of an, .. 39

innovations
corruption of some religions 105

integrity
natural human condition 39

intermediation
Holy Prophet's,..................... 59

Ishtihār Takmīl-e-Tablīgh
published by Promised Messiah[as] about conditions of *bai'at* ....:xix
ten conditions of *bai'at* published in, ... xix

istikhārah
defined.................................xiii
performing, before taking *bai'at* 7

Islām
aspect of human life and,.... 145
essence of the teachings of,. 139
establishing a beautiful culture of, ... 148

istighfār
be regular in, ... 62
defined xiii
to obtain strength perform, .. 66

J

Jamā'at
advice to the members of, ... 78
Allah's expectation from Jamā'at members, ... 41
Allah manifesting His glory through, ... 8
characteristics of members of, . 8
continues to be attacked by Satan, ... 151
defined xiii
distinction of, ... 160
duty of the members of, . 37, 85
established by Allah 40, 95
helping the poor 160
obedience to, fully mandatory .. 168
people who do not show patience, do not belong with, ... 41
prayer to serve humanity 161
purpose of joining, ... 36, 83
responsibilities of joining, ... 145
should continue to pray 152
showing patience 92
shun arrogance 130
treatment of poor by, ... 160
efforts to wipe out hunger .. 160
who enters into, ... 186

jealousy
a disease 80
ḥadīth on staying away from, ... 124
of one another 154

jizyah
abolishment of, ... 181
defined xiv

justice
truth and, ... 25

K

Khalīfah
defined xiv
will not ask anything against the Divine commandments or common sense 177

Khalīfatul Masīḥ I[ra]
shirk described by, ... 17
writings about feeding the hungry 159
writings about understanding of obedience 171

khilāfat
defined xv
system established by Allah 172
to last till the end of time ... 172

kindness
toward creation of Allah 145, 148

knowledge
search of, ... 154

kufr
defined xv
falsehood and, ... 22

L

land
unlawful occupation of, ... 35

lies
in trades, ... 32

love
perfect understanding is the root of, ... 144

loyalty
to government 42

lying
characteristic of a hypocrite .. 21
fire and, ... 22
in relation to children's upbringing 22
results in loss of credibility ... 23

M

Mahdī
defined xv
doctrine of bloody, ... 43

man/men
in need for heavenly light ... 128
mistreating their wives and children 121
modesty for, ... 30
no reason to be proud, ... 121
seek Allah with humility 128

Maulānā Nūr-ud-Dīn[ra]
first person to take *bai'at* of the Promised Messiah[as] 9

meekness
adopt, ... 86
arrogance and, ... 132
Holy Prophet's[sa] love for those who practice 134

Messiah
command of Allah to accept, ... 168

mischief
seek not, in the earth 39

modesty
for men and women, ... 30

moral qualities
known by height 38, 85

moral training
of children 22

morality
truthfulness and, ... 24

mosque
attending of 50

Movement
established by Allah............. 40
purpose of joining,......... 36, 83

Muḥammad[sa]
See Holy Prophet Muḥammad[sa]

Munshī 'Abdullāh
of Sanour[ra]
account of, *bai'at*, first 9

Muṣleḥ-e-Mau'ūd
writings about *khilāfat* and
Khalīfah........................... 172

Muslim(s)
covering faults of, ... 154
does not wrong his brother 154
every Muslims has six
obligations with regards to
other.............................. 153
false doctrines of, ... 43
not to think poorly of another,
.... 82
Prayer obligatory 53
suffering of a, are an expiation
for sins 91
sympathy for, ... 158

N

nation(s)
arrogance of,...................... 122
wicked and immoral, ... 33

nawāfil
offering of,.......................... 56

O

obedience
due to Allah alone 20
Muslims of the early era showed
examples of great,........... 177
necessary only in 'good
decisions' 174
superior example of,........... 177

P

Paradise
deeds leading to, ...22
glad tidings of,.................... 104
poor will enter five hundred
years earlier than others .. 157
six things assure entry into....28
tied to truthfulness 21

passion(s)
deluge of.............................44
Islāmic teachings in
restoring one's..................30
sacrificing of,.......................44
Satan and, ...44

patience
people who do not show, do
not belong to Jamā'at 41
real time to show, when tragedy
strikes...............................92

pauper
who is,................................35

perfect understanding
requires perfect love........... 144
what is,............................. 144

persecution
worse than killing................ 42

Pharaoh
arrogance of,..................... 125

physical work
means to attain chastity........ 27

poor
first one to enter Paradise
.... 157
helping of,........................ 160

Prayer
Aḥmadīs be free from arrogance
.... 125
comfort of eyes in,.............. 51
achieve concentration in,..... 55
children should offer, at the age of ten.............................. 49
essence and spirit of, lies in supplications.................... 52
establishment of five daily, ... 49
for Jamā'at members ....
.... 72, 118, 160, 186, 193
how to achieve concentration in,............. 55
importance of,.................... 53
justice to,........................... 53
neglecting a, will bring a man closer to apostasy and disbelief......................... 51
no concession in the matter of five daily,........................ 50
offering of,.......................... 52
offer five daily,..................... 86
obligatory on every Muslim .53
obligatory with no prerequisites..................... 53
observance of,...................... 50
to be free from obligation of,
.... 54
to keep the Jamā'at perfect
.... 152
what is 52

pride
characteristic of Satan......... 119
in *ṣalāt*............................... 127

Prophet of Islām
See Holy Prophet Muḥammad[sa]

Promised Messiah[as]
advice at the first *bai'at* 9
advice to Jamā'at to shun arrogance 130
commanded by Allah to take *bai'at* 6
death of the son of 6
defender of Islām...................5
defined..............................xvi
disliking that all type of people take his *bai'at*.....................6
first announcement regarding *bai'at* by, ...6
first *bai'at* taken by, ...9
humbleness of,.................. 120
obedience to, ... 168, 182
people request *bai'at* at the hands of the, ...5
purpose of taking *bai'at* by,.....7

taking first *bai'at* at the house of Ḥaḍrat Ṣūfī Aḥmad Jān 9
ten conditions of *bai'at* published by, ... xix
vulgar language used against, by *mullas* 183

Prophet(s)
can never give a command that is against the command of Allah 170
escape the hardships of this world and the hereafter by obeying, ... 172
will not ask against the Divine commandments or common sense 177

purdah
defined xvi
women enjoined to observe 106

Q

quarrels
take place over petty matters 80

R

Rabūbiyyat
attributes of Allah................ 16

rebellion
against government 42
safeguarding from the ways of, ...41

repentance
two types of, ...11

rights
two categories of, ...157
usurping of,..........................35

rituals
refrain from........................108
take one away from religion 106

rumours
people in habit of spreading 187

S

sacrifice
of the self..........................144

ṣadaqah
wealth does not decrease by giving,..........................133

salām
conveying *salām* of Holy Prophet Muḥammad[sa] to the Messiah and Mahdī 181
defined..............................xvi
emphasis in taking, of Holy Prophet Muḥammad[sa] to Messiah and Mahdī 181

use of, ... 153

Ṣalāt
alertness and promptness of, ... 142
arrogance and, ... 127
defined xvi
establishment of, ... 140
importance of, ... 138
pride in, ... 127

salvation
blood not needed for, ... 144
meaning of, ... 144
Unity of God and, ... 16

Satan
anger comes from, ... 83
arrogance of, ... 126–127
carnal passions and, ... 44
continues to attack the Jamā'at 152
exhibiting pride and arrogance 119
leading man astray 120
making men careless about his faith 10
pride, a characteristic of 119

self
sacrifice of 144

Shari'ah
Holy Qur'ān completes, ... 108

Sheikh 'Abdur-Raḥmān Khān
slaughtered in Kabul 98

shirk
a great sin 13
as not merely bowing before stones 14
defined xvi
described by Ḥaḍrat Khalīfatul Masīḥ I[ra] 17
falsehood and, ... 20
following one's desires, ... 14
forms of, ... 15
Holy Prophet Muḥammad[sa] feared, in his *ummah* 14
will not be forgiven 13

sick
visiting the sick an obligation 153

sin(s)
all forgiven except *shirk* 14
nine kinds of 19
ridding through certainty of faith 143
salvation from, ... 143
suffering of a Muslim are an expiation for, ... 91
three roots of, ... 123
with repentance all prior, forgiven 11

slave
man is a 61

social service
a good habit 153

steadfastness
show perfect 98
showed by 'Abdur-Raḥmān Khān[ra] 98

showed by Ṣāḥibzādah Sayyed 'Abdul Laṭīf Shahīd[ra] 98

streets
not a place of sitting............. 28

submission
under all circumstances 184

Ṣūfī Aḥmad Jan[ra]
first *bai'at* by Promised Messiah[as] taken at the house of,...................................... 9

supplications
essence of spirit of Prayer lies in 52

T

tahajjud
defined xvii
getting up for,...................... 57
incumbent for members to offer 57
offering of........................... 86

taqwā
defined xvii
light of,............................. 128
people of, ... 136

Tauḥīd
defined xvii
meaning of,.......................... 15

teachers
dedicated their lives for the service of humanity........ 161

truthfulness
believer speaks of, ...22
ḥadīth about,...................21, 28
justice and,...........................25
leads to Paradise 21–22
means to free from all sins 20
morality and.........................24
natural condition of man 23

tyrant
prayer of a............................34

U

'ulema
defined...............................xvii
worst of the creation 76

ummah
defined...............................xvii
Messiah will save the,......... 182

ungratefulness
to people.............................43

unity
three types of particularisation 16

V

veil
- Islāmic teaching on wearing, 29

vice
- refraining from, ... 29

W

walīmah
- defined xvii
- food wasted at.................... 102

waṣīlah
- defined .... xvii, 59

wealth
- charity does not reduce, ... 156
- does not decrease when spent in the way of Allah 134

wicked
- prayer of the, ... 34
- saving oneself from becoming 31
- will be in Hell...................... 32

wife
- waking up of for Prayers 57
- husband mistreating, ... 121

women
- enjoined to observe *purdah*. 106
- modesty for, ... 30
- prohibition against gazing at . 30
- taking pledge at the hand of Holy Prophet Muḥammad[sa] 4
- wearing the veil 29
- wickedness of, ... 32

world
- give faith preference over, .. 137

worship
- defination of......................... 17

Y

yarḥamukallāh
- use of, ... 153

Z

zakāt
- commandment of, ... 29
- defined................................ xvii
- giving of, ... 50, 140
- importance of, ... 138
- never fail to discharge obligation of, ... 52
- obligatory with certain prerequisites 53